T5-AXS-056

BEAUTIES ON MAD RIVER

Beauties
on Mad River

SELECTED AND NEW POEMS

Jan Conn

To Lisa – for being here –

My best wishes,

Jan

Slingerlands

Dec 10/08

SIGNAL
EDITIONS

SIGNAL EDITIONS IS AN IMPRINT OF VÉHICULE PRESS

ACKNOWLEDGMENTS

Some of these poems have appeared in *Arc Magazine*, *Antigonish Review*, *Event*, *Literary Review*, *Malahat Review*, *Matrix*, *New Quarterly*, and *Somewhere Across the Border*.
    For editorial comments on individual poems I warmly thank David Conn and Carl Schlichting. I am especially indebted to my editor Michael Harris. Michael Harris, Carl Schlichting and Ricardo Sternberg improved the Preface with their editorial suggestions.
    This book remembers, with love and great affection, two wonderful men: my friend and biologist Roberto Fabri Fialho, and my uncle Robert Hartley Conn.

Signal Editions Series editor: Michael Harris
Cover art and design: J.W. Stewart
Cover imaging: André Jacob
Photograph of the author: Carl Schlichting
Set in Perpetua by Simon Garamond
Printing: AGMV-Marquis Inc.

Copyright © Jan Conn 2000
Dépôt légal, Bibliothèque nationale du Québec and the
National Library of Canada, 4th quarter, 2000.

CANADIAN CATALOGUING IN PUBLICATION DATA

Conn, Jan, 1952-
Beauties on Mad River : selected and new poems

ISBN 1-55065-140-4

1. Title

PS8555.O543B43 2000   C811'.54   C00-901146-3
PR9199.3.C6375B43 2000

Distributed by General Distribution Services

Véhicule Press
www.vehiculepress.com

Printed in Canada on alkaline paper

for Carlo

Contents

EUCLID

LAMENT

THE LAND OF THE KINGFISHER

The title of each poem is followed by the book it appeared in: F - *The Fabulous Disguise of Ourselves*; s - *South of the Tudo Bem Café*; D - *What Dante Did With Loss*. Poems previously uncollected are denoted as N - New.

"She thought that sometimes you walk right into language as though it's a chair out of place in a dark room: a word, an expression you live with all your life can become suddenly, completely unfamiliar. That night Beatrice stumbled over death, but it was dark, and she was tired, and she believed that she had stumbled across love."

–Dale Peck

"For some things there is no cure.

There are distractions."

–Susan Mitchell

Preface

THE NEW POEMS in this collection have themselves suggested an unconventional organization of the book. Rather than in a simple chronological order, poems are arranged to portray the evolution of several themes that recur in my poetry. Thus, poems from several previous books may be clustered to follow the development of a particular theme. Each group of poems culminates with a more recent poem that draws the others into a pattern.

In contemplating the organization of this book, I drew on an analogy from both architecture and biology—the *keystone*. In architecture, a keystone is the uppermost and last stone set in an arch, completing it and locking its members together. In community ecology, a fascinating branch of biology, a keystone species is central or integral to the existence of the other species in that particular community. Each keystone poem is in a style inspired by the spirit of the eastern lyric form, the ghazal. Each is preceded by poems that felt antecedent to me, or that share a recurring image. Keystone poems are distinguished in the Contents by being separated from subsequent poems with a space.

As a means of understanding the choices of poems, as well as their order, let me illustrate the organizational scheme with a specific example. The section "Namesake," evokes a desert environment with images that not only draw one into that world, but especially into a particular quality of light I see, interiorly, and which I relate to the condition of mortality. The poems in this section share a foreshadowing of death or a sense of abandonment. In *Long Island, Summer, 1954*, I use the counterpoint of Marilyn Monroe's success and tragedy to dramatize my mother's suicide. Images of light also resonate throughout: the yellow of daffodils, burnished, golden and blonde. The word "light" is repeated, both for the quality of the sound of that specific word (as though it were a mantra that would force light to break through the imagined clouds) and to under-score the quality of light that permeates the poem.

In the Desert Air sets a scene on a balcony in an Egyptian or Lebanese town and then veers sharply into a vision of my mother dancing. Here the quality of light is alluded to by a different set of images: a desert flower, inner curtain, veil, white linen suit. The stereotypical Middle Eastern scene on a card, complete with mosque, palms, and yellowing desert air, is the focus of *To My Father at Age Nine*; it is liberated when the three men become my father and his brothers, and the light from the lantern illuminates both my mother's tragedy and some deeper understanding of my father. *Train. Camels. Sponges.* contrasts images of light and dark, and the camels are both emblematic (Lawrence's camels, kinetic statues) and real (they carry brides). The light is buttery (the golden dunes, the brass buttons), and functions as a contrast to the total darkness and deprivation of light (primal loss) far under the ocean.

Yellow Room distills these desert scenes and emotions in a stranger, more intense suite of images that culminates in a sense of loss that is still powerful yet calmer in some way, perhaps a little detached or remote. I have no way of knowing whether these keystone poems are the "final word" on the particular Conn-ic set of obsessions or view of the world that each one describes. Through the medium of the keystone poems, I perceive more clearly now, and in ways that I did not previously, the themes of individual earlier pieces—how each has been informed by now-familiar concerns and sets of images. These "plateau" pieces have functioned for me as true keystones, as revelatory glimpses back into my work of the last fifteen years.

Argentina

The Fifth Inhabitant of Mexico

for Jan Washburn

Emmylou Harris' blues
and Lyle Lovett's lyrics ricochet
around my room like firecrackers at a funeral.

Except that it's 4 AM and a red-eyed tree frog
is going to leap off the wall
into my fizzing grapefruit drink,
maybe swim around awhile,
maybe lip synch Lyle Lovett.

After all, the frog is looking decidedly sexy
in its green body suit, and me,
well, I'm kind of lonely,
a pushover for any amphibian, especially one
speaking fluent Spanish
from the rain forests of Costa Rica.

In the background of Frida Kahlo's
Four Inhabitants of Mexico,
hidden in the adobe houses and church,
in the damp shade, in the crevices,
were Mexican frogs—golden ones, poisonous ones,
ones that fit into the stunning speckled
mouth of an orchid, glass ones, ones with
red toes...

Hidden because they could see into the future
(Frida painted this picture in 1938),
the future
where they would become one of the mysterious
disappearing acts of the late twentieth century...

Amphibians are the Crown of the Evolutionary Tree!

If I ever get to heaven I'm not going in
unless the frogs are there first.

How to Think about Southern California

I fly alone across the continent—no strings attached.
From the dull green hurricanes of Florida
over the midwest and its dream of corn,
over the Grand Canyon and the white
vertebrae of snow-capped mountains.

To get to the Pacific
to think about you. And I do, but not in any way
you might imagine.

(Whatever you might feel, this is not
a love poem.)

II

I know, I know. Eucalyptus trees
are no longer politically or environmentally
correct because they're non-indigenous (like us),
displace native oaks, grow as fast
as bamboo. But they transform these sere landscapes
into mentholated heaven! And their cutlass-shaped
leaves cut the dry desert wind
into dusty ribbons of light.

Have you seen how the monarchs,
hundreds of them, cluster among the eucalyptus,
opening and closing their orange and black fans,
making whole groves levitate?

III

We had been walking for hours among creosotebush,
ocotillo, and cholla cactus. The light was
merciless, stunning. We had climbed huge granite boulders
and slithered back down them, finding hidden

blossoms in crevices, gall and scale insects
on every leaf and branch. It was mid-afternoon
and we were dehydrated, almost delirious.

Jocelyn saw the cattails first, then we all saw
the saffron willows, and the water—
shimmering, dark mineral blue—
and a flock of mallards, serenely paddling around
like theosophists.

One of the many delusions of the desert.

IV
These days I want only to emulate
the yucca night lizard
that lives its whole life
under the bark of a Joshua tree,
emerging at dusk, when the moon is full…

I am learning to love the tarantula, the
sidewinder, the long-legged kangaroo rat.
To preserve water in any form. To think of you
as an oasis I may only sip at
when in dire need.

Tell me everything you know
about the habits of the small burrowing owl,
the one Jesse James tamed and kept
on his shoulder to ward off bullets
and the evil eye.

In this landscape everything
is stripped away. It is where the cult of peyote
and the secrets of medicine women and men begin.
The light is confrontational. There is nowhere to hide
from yourself.

In the Red Hills

One by one, the crimson flames of cacti
are blown out. The soil in the Red Hills
is golden, ochre. Copper-coloured moonlight.

Ecstatic, you and I walked here years ago.
Among the dark stones, we found the shed skins
of hundreds of snakes, as though

celebrating some reptilian ritual.
High up, hawk
circled in the heat and we cut open a certain

species of cactus to drink the cool
vegetal water. I recall your obsession
with maps when we got lost somewhere

near Brownsville after midnight.
There were Christmas lights, golden tinsel,
the clamour of neon rodeo stars keeping our eyelids

bolted open. At such an hour the grocery store
with the stuffed moosehead, its mournful eyes
shining above the loud hum of the cooler.

We were exhausted. We drank Texas beer
and didn't sleep.
In the dark, I drove the car into a field of flowers.

How we ever made it into Mexico I've forgotten.

Enlightened Beings

When I left the hospital at eighteen in the humid Montreal summer they told me I was well but *there ain't no cure for the summertime blues*. So I wallowed, I wanted to be as lazy as a salt-water crocodile in Australia. A twenty-foot matron with no natural enemies except humans. Floating down the river, canoe plus paddles in one streamlined body, gliding among rough black boulders, diving down beneath the turquoise water to the sandy bottom—surfacing bleakly to being eighteen and female, in Montreal, looking for someone to give me an illegal abortion. *Look*, I said as calmly as possible, *that bastard who raped me in northern Ontario got me pregnant*. Worked week-ends in a bakery to reimburse the friend. Asphalt tormented me so I stumbled in the dried-out grass, bells attached to my back-pack to help me focus on the present, which was unbearably lonely and painful. Why not fantasies? I hike the worst face of Mt. Everest and save hundreds after an avalanche with my trusted standard poodle who believes she's a Saint Bernard. I discover in the rain forest of Pará a temple made of lace agate, and tell no one so it won't be ravaged by developers and criminals with greed as their credo. The crocodile fantasy though, that always gives me a great sense of personal power. I can always lunge toward my enemies and scare them into behaving like enlightened beings.

The Woman's Face Always Pressed Against the Window

This is how I live now.
Looking in on my life like a guest at a party.
Eating ginger snaps and drinking ice-cold
lemonade. Sitting on a balcony of stars.

Sometimes the moon sends me messages
through my giant fern. We commune.

I think of all the useless conversations I have been in,
feeling ethereal as smoke. Transparent.
Breaking down into the component parts.
Here a hand, there an ear, here a heart.
You can bury the hand in the mine in Asbestos,
the heart in Punta Arenas, and, as for the ear,
just throw it to the sharks off the east coast of Florida.
After all, I have been feeding on my fear of them for years.

When I lived in Caracas I watched movies every night,
mesmerized by melodrama and make-up. Thinking how many
locks were between me and the darkness.
Because I couldn't feel, I examined objects
and described them in notebooks in obsessive detail.
I recall an orchid, for example, that went on for days.
I stuck glow-in-the-dark stars on the ceiling
and invented new constellations every night
to the sound of gunfire from the *barrios*
that surrounded the house.
Always a feeling of bravado and desperation
in the pollen-filled air I inhaled every minute
like an asthmatic.

Arizona

I

So close to Mexico we can hear the mariachi bands
practice in the plaza, late afternoon sun burning

both sides of the border equally. If the sun made a sound
it would be a dial tone, noisy and irritating.

What I crave is the scarlet light from the ocotillo flowers,
the fallen petals dragged one by one underground

to illuminate the tunnels of the fierce brown desert ants.

II

Over the next rise a hill made of white quartz,
same stillness and poise as polished marble,

the pink and rose-coloured seams glorious in some arcane way,
like someone who's lived through too much sorrow, and can't contain

the anguish at the end. It spills over.

San Juan Bautista, with Magenta Anthuriums

The night we arrived in Yaguaraparo, *la reina* was chosen,
at three in the morning, not for her beauty or bearing,
but for her skill in catching and cooking a succulent variety

of land crab, which all the judges had to taste several times
before crowning her with magenta anthuriums. This place
is famous for its hand-painted murals of creatures

from the sea beyond us, and beyond the mangroves
at the ragged edge of town. We catch a whiff
of that stale salty smell, the pungent aftermath

of love-making in a small hotel room with a ceiling fan
which lulls everybody else but me to sleep—
no matter how delicious the idea of self-

perpetuating breeze. Following the newly-crowned queen
down rain-slicked streets, people burst into dance
spontaneously, their bodies supple as serpents.

The statue of *San Juan Bautista* glows a faint blue
from the light cast by row upon row
of flickering indigo candles.

I wake days later, it seems, alone in a hammock,
in the courtyard of a deserted house. High, lovely
wooden ceilings. Muted green. Pillars someone has kindly attached

my colourful hammock ropes to. Silver streaks of rain
that alternate with the gloomy light filtering
between the slender leaves of mango trees.

The flowers of *Syzygium*, their fuchsia petals
prodding me languidly awake, and the ripened mangoes,
falling at random onto the rain-soaked, blackened earth.

On the Other Side of Love

Ah, my difficult daughter, sighs my mother,
rising one more time from the dead,
an apparition among the fireflies and incessant violet
flashes of lightning over Casigua,
above the purple flowering *apamate* and palm trees,
above the wood smoke and smell of lemons
and urine and lime trees...

You're going to burn out
like the flaming bucaré blossoms.

I admit I'm consumed by loss—
though I want something larger.
For example, the *Virgen de Coromoto*
could levitate from her new shrine at Guanaré
and walk on tiptoe
down the broken spine of the *Cordillera*,
flirting with the snow-clouds
gathering over *Pico Bolívar*,
distributing free *lotería* tickets
to every woman and child in Venezuela.

That would cheer me up, at least temporarily.

To have k.d. lang sing *Crying Over You* or
The Yellow Rose of Texas. That would cheer me up too,
except that I live in Florida.

My mother flaps down impatiently, settling
like a semi-precious stone
among the egrets. *I'm getting rather faint*, she says.
And it's true, I can see through her body,
all the way across the Maracaibo Basin,
past the haciendas and saman trees,
the smoldering sugar cane fields, the ponds
mirroring rain clouds and white water lilies:

I dream of making love to a woman
and then the gorgeous head
of a horse-like creature
emerges from the earth
covered with calla lilies and red hibiscus.

There should be a *Virgen del Cebú* here.
What's worshipped is pasture grass
and beef by the kilogram, an occasional rodeo star,
and a man who claims to cure hoof and mouth disease
by playing an ancient saxophone beneath a ceiba tree
every afternoon around five o'clock
in the plaza in *El Vigía*.

What do I want? The satin texture of your skin,
your tongue in my mouth,
your body
curled around mine like a snail.

Make love to me in this hammock, make love to me
on the roof of the *Hotel las Hermanas*,
make love to me among the bruised orange blossoms...

Do you realize I drove all the way from Caracas
in the back of a jeep
with two hyacinth macaws
that recited Gabriela Mistral and César Vallejo
in alternating voices
and refused to eat anything but *arepas* and *cambures*?

I'm not looking for delirium or hallucinations.
Something on the other side of love, a parallel
universe, a way out, a way
back in: the gas fires at night lighting
southwestern Zulia, the dark drums of San Benito,
the way the air resonates at noon like a plucked guitar,
the sadness of the mud banks
of the *Río de Oro*.

Sexta Avenida

Moon eats the leaves of eucalyptus
each night climbing a little higher.
The *avenida* erupts into sound:
the hard barking of dogs.

The post office in pink and white
is a birthday cake with candles of glass
but the walls are being absorbed
by the rain, the voice
of a thousand forgotten summers.

Bluebird on the roof, black bees
huddled in the velvet-tongued hibiscus.
Under dark skies the beggars
look almost beautiful.

Salvaterra

At the end of the road is the pale blue film
of the sea. The waves keep dreaming themselves
awake, in a calm place, like the Sahara,
but this never happens.

The girl, yellow flowers braided into her hair,
sells us the first rains of the dry season.
All day the red earth washes slowly
into the mouth of the sea.

I wanted a place to begin again, a lagoon, not this
sleepy town where the electrical generator chugs
all night, turning over and over in its sleep
the little shivers of electricity
surging down the dove-grey walls of my room.

The plantation owner tempts me:
beautiful sandy beaches, long nights
awash with soft waves and sentimental Brazilian music.

Beneath dark palms, a blind girl croons to herself
by the white ruins of the Art Museum
while drunken men race water buffalo around and
around the plaza in the rain.

By a Line of Eucalyptus

On the roadside, a single black shoe
huddles in the white dust.
Vultures scrabble over the shreds of a snake.

Everyone in the northeast—Ceará, Paraíba,
Pernambuco, Alagoas—worships the god of rain.
Day after cloudless day he doesn't
show his face. Thunderheads built up.
The air is turquoise, electric.

Behind the dazzling yellow cucurbit flowers
a dark woman in a blue dress
bends into the dry arms of maize.

Release is the dead lizard
slung on the back of a man whose skin
brings the dry herb smell of the *caatinga*
to his family.

Dust on his gun, his small
woven hunting bag. The story
of a pink cactus blossom beside
the sleeping lizard. Later,
the sapphire belt of Orion overhead,
lightning bugs pulsing the empty field.

About Pará

for Roberto Fabri Fialho

1. Watch for the green lightning bugs and when you count to three between flashes it will rain.

2. The fish in Tartaralguzinho are mercury-filled and sold in the market as thermometers.

3. The eye of God is equal parts green, hazel, agate, earth brown and black at midnight.

4. The best way to deal with the sudden rash that signals a heat wave is to dream continuously of snow falling in empty fields.

5. Açaí palm ice cream tastes like grass or earth (my husband loves it though).

6. There are some problems with the plumbing. (Don't drink the water.)

7. The women who work in the canning factory in Cametá put twice the recommended dose of salt in the hearts of palms in homage to the Virgin of Nazaré to remind them of her tears.

8. Eye of dolphin is the most expensive aphrodisiac in the *Ver-o-Peso* market in Belém.

9. Elis Regina didn't die of an overdose of whiskey and cocaine—she's alive and well and living in Macapá. We saw her on the beach at midnight dancing beneath the moons of Jupiter. Someone stole her vocal cords.

10. If you eat *manisoba* you'll be awakened by dreams of short women attacking each other with tangerines.

Incident, Brazil

The girl wraps hearts of palm in a banana leaf.
That's not the way we do it at home, complains

the grandmother, recently arrived from Ireland.
The banana flower is purple and voluptuous

and if you stare at it too long when the moon is full,
you'll give birth to deformed children.

At night, the grandmother moonbathes in a black bathing suit,
frosted mottled skin, glazing on a wedding cake.

Ireland in July is plump and shining and the eyes of God
linger long on its luscious fields.

I wish I'd never come, she says to her daughter-in-law.

She gives her papaya with lime for her digestive
complaints and secretly feeds her tiny pieces of paper

on which are written, *Go home, your house is on fire...*

In a Black Wind

We crouch in the courtyard
where a wind picks up
a few last rain drops and dusty
papaya leaves, driving them
against a white plaster wall.

This is the day of the Festival of Soldiers
and military planes fly low overhead
celebrating more than a year in power
without a successful coup. You ask me
what I'm thinking.

Last week in Panajachel I heard
the firing squad, wanting to believe
in firecrackers.

I was in the garden. A group of children
arrived at the gate.
They told me a man was dead in the street.
On his feet are expensive shoes.

Hibiscus fell during the night
onto his dark shirt and hair.
Someone dragged him
down a dirt road by his heels.

I went down to clean my hands
in the lake still black as the road
to the north in the *Popul Vuh*

or all the bars on windows
behind which faces are peering out,
faces that slowly flicker out,
candles in a black wind.

El Amparo

When it's dry,
everything flowers.
Small bushes, not listed in any guide.
A twisted tree, blackened as charcoal.
You don't expect to hear hot jazz
blown through the pale orange lips
of the trumpet flowers—but a lament,
slow, half-heard, dirge
of *la epoca seca*.

The fence posts cut last season
have blossomed into two-metre trees,
branches and leaves tossing in the hot morning wind
like a horse trying endlessly to rid itself of flies.
And the poinsettia bracts
scattered here and there across the hills,
how they resemble crimson tailfeathers!

The ripeness of coconuts! Yellow globules, incandescent.
You expect at night
to be guided by their glimmer, warm as candles.
The slick smooth yellow trunks of bamboo.
Countless green textures of leaves.

A few red African tulip petals scattered
along the roadside.
Small scarlet pools
like the bodies of the fishermen
murdered in *El Amparo*.

Shot by members of the army, above the law,
unaccountable.

Lowland tropical forest,
hawks ride the updrafts toward the *Cordillera*,
and far below women wash rainbows in the muddy pools
of a drying riverbed.

Beside them, mustard-yellow flowers,
dense and luxuriant,
weigh down the whole valley with their fragrance.

Two Paintings of Lily Pads

One, jade on charcoal, stark, precise.
It's midnight on the pond
or the painter emerging
from three days of alcohol
about to be overwhelmed by a hint of pink,
a bud, a woman's sex freeze-framed.

Opposite, pastels immersed
in soap-bubbled light, vague impressions,
the light much as it is now,
late afternoon, diffuse,
so the lily pads are merely
projections of themselves,
underdeveloped negatives.

After dusk, the gravel causeway to Flores,
an egret's wing balanced on black water.
The lake's membrane pulled tight
except at the edges, where it riffles—

letting go the trapped gas,
the intricate lives of micro-organisms.
Lily pads undulate,
landing pads for minute spaceships,
origin of these bizarre frogs,
in pairs, like hand-cuffs,
found nowhere but this lake.

We read about their delicate
nervous system, their mating habits,
a pornography of speckled, iridescent skin.

Their music swells the lavender sky,
breaking in on the painter's sleep.
He rolls over, cursing.
He would like to shoot
the frogs' pale bellies,
watch them splatter the lake.

He would also shoot the moon
for coming into his room uninvited
and making the woman's skin
glow like pearls, like the unprotected
side of a fish.

He pushes his penis into her
to shut out the raucous frogs,
their uninhibited couplings.

Letter Home After Living Six Months in Caracas

I am at loose ends
waking from dreams of lost language,
stuttering in French and very bad Spanish.

Too many days with only the company
of books on Antarctica, a Japanese novel,
and the sad story of *The Wide Sargasso Sea*.

Too much fuel, not enough fire.

Right hemisphere to left hemisphere, do you read me?

Chile is "free"
but Nicaragua is a "threat."
Mexico vigorously denies AMNESTY reports.
Former president Lusinchi departs for Miami.
I go to study mosquitoes and malaria in La Lengüeta.

In Canada the leaves turn gold and amber and scarlet
and cinnamon
but here the poinsettias year round
bleed brilliantly.

One small apartment in San Bernardino (with balcony)
can contain the world
or reject it.

I'm living on black olives and salted almonds.

Surely this affects my poise?
Ma poèsie?
The fragile internal balance of things?

There is no place to be calm in this city.
I'm the firefly caught in our field station in Guaquitas
blinking off/on, off/on.

Paul Horn is inside the Taj Mahal (lucky man).
I'm inside nothing, a bubble of air.

The sun penetrates in brief long lances,
which I parry,
leaving me the clouds, a poor victory.

Is there anything the matter?

: a dying rat on the sidewalk yesterday, twitching,
surrounded by the purple slippers of bougainvillea;
my tiger oven-mitts bite down hungrily
not on antelopes but on air.

The Empire of Snow

for Ellen Moore and Scott Harrison

The hills look smoked. A fine permanent haze
to which the eyes never adjust.

Icicles along the edge of a small twisting creek.
The water serpentine or light blue, moving over ice
or soundlessly beneath it,
over buried leaves, toads estivating in the thick
brown mud, trout slipping beneath the roots
of trees...

Gorgeous yellow snow willows. Rocks
half-buried like a koan. The zen of an avalanche.
A whole hillside of white candles, flickering:
numinous beings in the guise of trees.

The black dog snuffling through deep snow,
following faint trails of rabbit, red fox, mouse,
whiskers iced in a parody of wax-tipped moustache,
all at once shooting up out of drift
into tourmaline light and snow shadows
like a muskrat or otter surfacing.

The tall tawny grasses,
heads above the drifts, casting mauve shadows
the colour of eyelids.

And in the fields, after the children
have had their energies bundled indoors,
and the late afternoon shadows
seem at a loss,

the asymmetrical snow angels they've made
glow
like the after-image of a large white moth

or a dead baby from a *barrio* in Caracas I saw
dressed as an angel
in a coffin the size of a large man's shoe.

Into the Gathering Dark

A woman and a man drive a rented car
hundreds of kilometres through northern Guatemala
into the gathering dark, foolishly, intently,
the woman driving too quickly, the man

unable to speak of the few things he has come
to value. He watches a white stallion
tethered by the dusty roadside, its matted hair
suddenly coral-coloured as the sun
plunges behind a jagged line of mountains.

Between him and the stallion, nothing.

A hologram of flies.

On both sides of the road the fields
look blasted: clotted soil, dry flutter of maize.

They have taken this turn-off
because several drunken men
crowded around a tiny wooden building
pointed this way. This way to Colomba

and the highway where ten years ago a truck
drove off the road, killing the passenger instantly.
The passenger who was the brother
of this man in the car

which explains their urgency but not
the violence, rushing to meet them
in the form of stones hurled at the car windows
by the inhabitants of a small *pueblo*
because they are strangers
who could easily bring more deaths with them,
or because the stabbing white headlights

of the white rental car
might be used to extract information
by men who probe the soft inner reaches
of women
and the genitals of men
by night.

Argentina

Tronador Mountain closes its door. I ride an avalanche
into a jade crevasse but springtime

never comes. Cobalt ice in solid sheets, blocks
of frozen water the size of icebergs.

Crystals mystics would covet. Send me a compass flower;
send me a rose. Follow the compass to the bright

streets of Buenos Aires, over the inhaled breath
of the pampas, let me lie down in that long

long grass. Sip tea through a silver sieve, watch
a knife fight where no one, miraculously, gets killed.

I'll cruise down the wide boulevards, collide
with the Mothers, signs ragged, flowers frayed,

still marching for their lost children and husbands
while Robert Duvall practices dancing the tango.

NAMESAKE

Fusion

Without a knock
or chiming of bells,
a man appears in our house
beside the dark red table.
He intends to murder one of my parents.

I want to know which one.

I wake from this recurring dream,
I'm 12 years old.
I think he wants my adolescent body
untouched, raised in an atmosphere
too rich for normal growth,
humid and decadent.

What I understand of sex
is gleaned from a book about anglerfish.
The male of some species,
thumbnail-size, finds a large female
the same way a shark can detect
a drop of blood
in a million parts of seawater.

He finds her and attaches
with a few specialized teeth,
fusing fishscale to fishscale.

As the eldest daughter
I worship
my father, the man who taught me
to paddle a canoe in a storm
while he sat in the bow
and read *Scientific American*,

not my mother, her dark hair
curled around one finger
as she sleeps in the warmth of the cottage,
her face toward the row of maples
outside the window.

She says when it's dry she'll go collecting bullrushes
while her children, alone on the summer veranda,
invent alternatives for the word love.

One View from the Look-Out Tower

This isn't a town you drive through
to get to somewhere more interesting.
It's a full stop, like the full moon,
from far away, mysterious and luminous,
up close
like the real moon,
it's hard and cold
and strewn with piles of lifeless grey rock.

Driving toward it at night
the open-pit mine radiates
a particular blackness, alive
with mineral knowledge, compelling.
As a teen-age girl I could stand
on the front lawn and feel it press against
the whole length of my body, insatiable.

I stand on the silver
look-out tower, an adult woman,
and think that this is where you really died.
Florence Elliot Cole Conn.
Not in Denver, Colorado, in 1976,
locked in a garage with the car motor running
but here, in Asbestos, you died many times, in secret,
and none of us recognized the intricate darkness
that held you like a blacksmith
forging some hard and beautiful metal into a shape
that couldn't endure the bending.

The Man with My Mother's Hands

is here again, at the door, greeting me,
I want to buy a brand-new used car, and he has
a whole basement full of them.
Every shade you can imagine! Magenta,
lemon-yellow, creamy white, the colour of violets,
of bluebird eggs, malachite, sandstone!

But first I must pass through the garden labyrinth
without getting lost. He takes my hand,
but his hand is my mother's hand, with coral
nailpolish on long tapered nails, and this hand
has a will of its own. Soon I am flying
over the garden, looking down at its intricate paths,
dead-ends of poison oak and brambles, the circular trails
through scarlet poppies and drowsiness, the stinging
nettles in amongst the roses...

And then I go down into the basement
where there's a white piano in one corner
on which I must somehow play a brilliant composition
which I cannot do
but then my mother's hands descend
down the stairs behind me and begin to skim
across the notes, two wild swallows
sounding like the wind dancing with leaves in autumn
or the stars humming during daylight, when they think
no one can hear them

and I am nearly ready to see the cars

but a young girl wearing red felt shorts
with real stars sewn into them
looks up from her drawing
and asks me about the goblin
in the next room beneath the coffee table.

The goblin is black and formless and she is not afraid of it
but I am terrified. My mother's hands rush in
but they are swallowed up. The car salesman follows.
The girl and I sit down near the goblin
and begin to tell it a story...

When You Were Ours

In the summers at our cottage, the wooden cottage
designed by our father, with huge picture windows
facing the water, and a deck,
and a 30-ft sailboat parked up beneath the house
on a railway flatcar, then
we had you all to ourselves.

Your mother sailed to England as she would do
every summer until her death, and your husband came
from the city only on week-ends.
So you were ours.

These are the only pictures of us I can bear to look at,
even now, so many years later. All of us swimming,
picking raspberries, climbing up into the treehouse,
walking home in the pitch blackness without a flashlight,
finding our way by touch
and the delicate odour of night-blooming flowers,
knowing you were up, waiting, knowing
that huge unspoken love, which was nearly ready to burst,
was waiting, and because you couldn't communicate
feeling, we learned to read you
as a blind person will read scent and sound,
we anticipated your love,
we knew it had to be somewhere,
what mother could have borne these five children
and not loved us
until death do us part.

Learning to Be My Father's Daughter

At twelve, my brother would put on a driver's cap
and climb up into the bulky black Chevrolet.
He was the chauffeur,
he'd drive us out of Asbestos,
all the way to San Francisco.

One trip I had him stop the car.
It was hot, midsummer,
the car was a black oven
and we were baking, jammed into the back seat,
myself and my three sisters.

I clambered up onto the roof
and my brother was suddenly
there behind me, he threw me off
onto the pavement
the way you'd toss a sack of rice
down, just to see the grains, white and
polished, pour out of the split burlap.

I saw blood on my elbows & knees.
I remember screaming and then
there was my father, his calculations
of the prices of mining stocks disturbed,
he picked me up and dangled me, *don't cry*,
shook me like a mop, *it doesn't hurt*,
told me how he learned to control
the pain of an abscess when he was only 15
by imagining it elsewhere, outside his body.

When my mother was airlifted
from the garage filled with carbon monoxide,
registered at the hospital DOA,

and my father had her cremated
before her children arrived, refusing
a funeral, I didn't even whimper,
I took that pain and pushed it as far outside my body as I could,
I watched it dangle in space beside my father's pain,
quite separate, those two pains, although
they were father and daughter.

A Tapestry

Backs to the miniature pear-trees
in the medieval herbal garden,
my sister and I goof around,
teen-aged. The pears muscular
as green uteri, unpicked,
untasted.

The leaves are locked in resin
as though in a museum for extinct trees.
Above them our mother sits, cross-legged
on a satin cloud, surrounded
by a crowd of women. She's talking
to us through a loud-speaker,
she's saying, *Have you killed her yet,*
the impostor, the new wife? Have you learned
how to torture your father?

Fighting the drone of a plane
that writes a message in the sticky
blue-seamed sky over the Hudson,
mother talks louder,
her dead mother joins her and then
an image of her only son, alone
among all those women.

It's for him I let go
of my sister's hand, climbing up
on the stone wall
warmed by September,
past the comfrey and gold of pleasure,
St. John's wort and fennel seed,
the nuns building gigantic nests,
the tombs of the crusaders.

While I was Looking at the Background You Walked Out of the Picture

I've sent you a tiger.
Its fur burns intense orange,
radiant against the dark. Plants around it
send up volleys of smells, fantastic.

Its ears are filled with white hair,
moth antennae
bent in and listening to dreams
of the rain forest: fat frogs creaking,
a prey of insects crackling.

You leave me behind, always,
coming home months later, from India,
Africa, Colombia—with another
smell on your skin, a suitcase
of saris and ivory elephants for your wife,

and smaller gifts for us, the daughters, growing
like Hallowe'en pumpkins, awkward teeth
stuck in our grins.

I decide to become an archaeologist,
to go where you've been
while the scent is still fresh.

Letter to My Mother on the Anniverary of Her Suicide

I used to want you to come back into our lives
but now if I saw you hesitating on a streetcorner,
buying fabric at a woolen outlet, slowly raking
autumn leaves or planting the tulip bulbs
that would bloom
crimson and magenta
in the back garden all spring,
I would run as fast as I could
and get a gun,
a silver one inlaid with mahogany and teak,
well-handled, well-oiled, used
by other abandoned children,
and I would hold it at your temple,
where your thick black eyebrows rose and fell
like blackbirds throughout my childhood,
where your lovely white earlobes held
in the glitter of your exotic earrings
all the beauty I had access to,
behind which your anguish
demolished you, and then, without hesitation,
demolished all of us, five children
and a husband, I would level that gun
without a pause, without listening to you
beg for mercy or understanding,
I would stand very straight
and think of the years of obsession,
I would think of the ruin of our lives,
I would pull the trigger
and I would say,
This is my life
and I will live it
as far away from your shadow as I can.

The Darker Blue Inside

I keep in my room in Caracas
my mother's olive-coloured vase from China,
the background etched with a repetitive black pattern
like families of snail shells found in a mountain stream
and lined up in rows as a child might do
learning to count
with an abacus.

This is what my mother saw, one of the last things,
and she had been reading that enigmatic book
The French Lieutenant's Woman that must have made her
ache for her life
or for the life she hadn't chosen.

Inserted in front of the wall of snails
is a pink flowering branch—
each flower shaped like a cloud,
each cloud drifting above a gorge,
the gorge suggestive of limitlessness—

and circling the half-moon lid
is a simple design in a shade of turquoise
that isn't quite believable
as, 14 years later, her death still isn't.

My sister used to insist
one day my mother would stroll back into our lives
twirling a parasol
like a vision from a distant century
having been merely lost to us for a while
and now returned as a gift
better than before—

but I take off the lid
and look at the darker blue inside,
someone's imagined Chinese heaven
full of dragons, monkeys, snakes, wild boars…

What I see is a solitary woman, slumped
on a leather car seat. The leather polished and dark.
One of her hands clenched into a fist.
The other loose, open, in surrender or
supplication.

Inscrutable, her body.
Not yet decomposed.
The hair unmussed. The watch on the wrist
ticking without pause. Silver earrings still warm
from the recent warmth of her body.
The temperature dropping now in the unheated garage.
The snow outside falling and falling.

Her lipstick "Wild Plum," a perfect
outline of her lips.
As though she had applied it
in the rear-view mirror, clicked shut the tube,
dropped it into her purse, taken out the keys,
turned on the ignition…

How long did she pause?
Did she think of us? Did she remember
her mother, who lived with us all those years,
or her father, who died the same year
her first child was born?

Then she would have started to inhale the gas,
not knowing precisely how long it would take
to feel drowsy, to feel warm…
In her warm coat, fur-lined boots, wearing a scarf,
an ordinary scarf, suffused
with her favourite perfume *Caleche*…

One Version of Myself at Three

I was thinking how Van Gogh's ear
ended up in the movie *Blue Velvet*
and simultaneously multiplied by hundreds
like dried pears or apples
in a Carolyn Forché poem, in any case
listening in, tuned to the earth.

Perhaps Van Gogh saw light waves
continuously, different ones vibrating for
every shade and nuance of colour.
Imagine navy, delft, ultramarine,
turquoise, cadmium—dancing in the sky
all day and night, even with your eyes
shut. Unable to filter out anything
extraneous. Dazzling and constantly
overwhelming. Well.

Insomnia's not like that. It's the palm trees
in my bedroom that keep prodding me awake,
thinking in long green pulses
of Brazil.

Or the black and white photograph of myself
at three, gleefully swinging higher and higher
in someone's backyard in Montreal West,
il y a longtemps. Little checked flannel shirt,
blue and red and black, and blue corduroy pants
with matching checked cuffs, you know the kind.

A rope swing with a wooden seat and behind me
in the background is a snake charmer
intently playing a flute, keeping
the ropes miraculously suspended in the air.

Behind All the Walls There are Gardens

Behind all the walls
there are gardens, flowers in exile.
The family that lives
in their presence
doesn't see them anymore,
but every time they go out,
their retinas playback minute images,
dancing at the edges of sight.

The oldest boy is a mixture
of trumpet flowers and narcissus,
adolescent, almost drowning
in the palpable confusion of girls.
When one plants a kiss on his cheek
it grows there untended,
so the next time he sees her,
his whole face sweats
the same colour as her lips.
He doesn't have enough pockets
for all his hands.

He'd like her to explain things to him,
but the girl only knows
what her bones know,
lengthening and curving,
and she'd tell him
if she knew how,
but it's not what he needs to hear.
He's baffled by his own voice,
it betrays him,
and everything he touches
falls apart in his fists,
random violence
no one can tell him about.

The girl, though, she knows what it means
to be associated
with the amethyst of evening,
when her friends go home
to the gardens their families are
and the perfume dopes them,
they can't behave
the way they do outside.

She stays out late and later,
daring the night
the way a girl will
when she's feeling brave and defiant
& her mother's face
is a bright blur on the horizon,
flickering in and out of sight,
sheet lightning,
or the way her stomach feels
when she pushes herself too far.

She knows what her brother's friends
want, they'd pin her on their lapels
if they could, and brag about her colour,
the way she glistens.

Chibougamau

All summer the teen-age daughter
mooned over a boy named John, away
at summer camp. Each day she would
put on the white silk blouse and creamy
cashmere sweater with what she thought of as her
"good flannel pants" and stroll along the dirt road
past rows of summer cottages until she reached his.
Dark green with a screened-in porch

and she couldn't see anything inside.
Earlier in the summer they went to the pool hall
down the road to drink beer and play the pinball machine
and kiss in corners where mosquitoes bite.

She stood in front of his house for hours, twisting the cheap
gold-plated ring he'd given her around and around
her middle finger to make him appear.
Her parents thought her "difficult" and "not especially

nice to be around" but what she wanted
was a father who would take her to Chibougamau
to make a survey of igneous rock or to India
to assess a mine in exchange for a tiger hunt and
an ivory replica of the Taj Mahal. She
practiced yoga diligently and asked her father over breakfast
to recite *Om Mani Padme Hum* and whether his
sexual *chakra* was filled with early morning energy yet.

Mid-Summer, 1968

I follow this car along a dirt road
out to the lake. It's the kind of night
it would be easy to shift gears & accelerate
into orbit around Saturn.
Beautiful cold blue space.

The boy drives with one hand.
The other groping the girl
curled up next to him.
Either she wonders what's taking him so long
or she's terrified, but lulled anyhow
by the alcohol that they've
both been drinking.

Soon they'll park near the lake's edge,
the girl lost in the plush upholstery
as the boy's breathing
slide-trombones past her ear.

She likes his face
outlined against the submarine
lights of the dashboard,
his cock hardening as it moves
along the flank of her jeans,
that anything could happen.

I know this scenario.
I get out of my car and go
to the open window she's hunched against.
I touch the back of her neck.
She lifts her head
but her eyes look up past me
to the moon where it floats
like the bathing cap of a swimmer
crossing the Atlantic.

Flight

for Phil Lounibos

Sitting on the runway in Pittsburgh, waiting to be de-iced. Like de-icing, with the tongue, the elaborate cakes we had for birthday parties when I was in boarding school, age fifteen. Chocolate chip with marshmallow and pistachio-nut frosting. Orange-pineapple cake topped with plastic cherries. Snowing hard in Pittsburgh. Well, I'm off to Florida. To the sun and dreamy time, ambling along the beach, lying in the shade of palm and hibiscus. Maybe I'll bring back to wintry Vermont a basket of oranges, mandarins and tangelos. All those cakes, week after week. The cooks and the pastry chef indulging a whole school full of homesick, spoiled, angst-ridden girls. And one night a girl ran away, across the dark fields, and I looked out my shared bedroom window, out onto the rough grey and silver stones, shining in the moonlight. The castle rock from *Wuthering Heights* just there, above the school, framed in darkness. The tiny being with white wings looked solemnly back at me from its home in the moist green moss. The moonlight deepened. The girl kept running.

Namesake

In the red wooden box, elaborately carved,
lived all our family secrets. As a teen-age

girl, I pilfered the box and opened it in private.
Inside, a smaller red box. Letters from Aunt Emma,

my namesake, "to whom" inked out, black as midnight.
About her spiritual quest, her dismissal

from the convent age eighteen for falling in love
with the moon. Silver stigmata appearing

at the wrong time and place. *Marry me*, she wrote
to the moon. *Bring me to Babylon. Give me silk*

and satin wings that I might greet you fittingly.
All day I drink Bloody Marys to commemorate

her death by poison, her pioneering
flight to the moon.

Carthage

Here, he said, pointing at the detailed map, *here*
is where Carthage lay then. Hannibal

had it made. Geology contributed too, of course.
Red stone, black canyon walls, swamps and marshes

in which men and horses and elephants
simply disappeared. He paused, considering

my face. *You aren't consumed by history, I*
can tell. Why are you here? Are you married?

No, I smile, *but my Aunt Emma*
was engaged to the moon. We look at it out the curtainless

window as it rises on yellow stilts
above the ruins of Carthage.

Long Island, Summer, 1954

I was two years old in 1954
when Norma Jean sat poised
on the metal bar of a children's
roundabout, the kind that used to make me
dizzy and sick when I spun it out-of-control
faster and faster, hanging from one thin bony arm—
but that was much later, after she was already dead.

Now she wears for the photographer
a striped sleeveless top
the colour of daffodils and black roses,
tiger lilies and the soft pillow-white
of the white narcissus,
holding a copy of James Joyce's *Ulysses*,
showing the whole glorious length of her
flawless legs—burnished, we might say—radiant,
golden, perfect legs. Not a single blemish or scar.

Not for me to say whether or not
she was reading with great attention
because she was in a child's playground in Long Island,
distracted by the photographer, the light,
deep in the middle of her heroic and tragic life,
no end in sight,

and I was in a small provincial town in southeastern Québec
learning to walk, not yet aware
of James Joyce or Marilyn Monroe
or death by suicide.

That was all far off, in the future,
in another country
and I was safe in my mother's arms
as in a fortress of blood, muscle, and singing bone,
a fortress under siege from within,

but this is not apparent in 1954
any more than Norma Jean's wavering descent
is visible in her calm, sleepy, golden body,
her short bleached blonde hair

or the glossy leaves of the trees
behind her in the park singing,
Light. Light. Light.

In the Desert Air

As you rise, the sweat on your chest after love-making
catches the shimmering of the desert air south of El Faiyum.
Palm trees outside embedded in perlite,
stranded on your balcony.
The scent of a flower
that blooms once every hundred years.

Behind the white-and-green drapes
there is an inner curtain, sheer
as a veil, against which, in silhouette,
your body is a dream I once had
of my mother waltzing in an ankle length gown
with some man in an empty room.

I hear her shoes scrape the floor
lightly, the sigh of her dress
as it brushes her stockings.

She dances with an image
of her husband at 24,
the year he went into the navy.
His black moustache lends him a gallant air
which he lost somewhere in the Mediterranean
when his ship was torpedoed.

She dances with the man she thought
she had married. She dances with the ghost
of her father, moving formally,
in a white linen suit
and indigo bow-tie
holding his daughter
whom he doesn't remember
an arm's length away from his body.

To My Father at Age Nine

A slender boy of nine,
green eyes flecked with gold,
a summer meadow in full sunlight.
A boy who sends a card to his grandmother
on Mother's Day. He says she'll be lonely,
with her children gone, grown-up.
Alone in her echoing house by the lake.
His narrow face glimmers
as he writes.

On the front of the card are three men.
Two stand deep in conversation
on the stone steps of a mosque.
The third walks with a lantern
toward a body of water. In the background
are palms and yellowing desert air
crisp as a parchment.

This is my father who will leave his two brothers
and the haven of Toronto in the 50s
for a small Québec town in *les Cantons de l'Est*.
He will take along his young wife, but she
isn't in this picture, she will have been erased
by the darkness which seeped into her body,
invisible, made her invisible.

The lantern illuminates the man's bones
like an x-ray or an obscure biological diagram.
He, the boy, cannot see beyond that.

Train. Camels. Sponges.

Clickety-clack. Clickety-clack. Mesmer. Mesmerizing.
Eyelids getting heavier and heavier.

What was that you were saying?
Something about camels.
They were in a hurry.
Were they coming or going?
I remember now. They were Lawrence's camels,
being ridden over golden dunes,
endlessly rocking in the buttery light.
Kinetic statues. Endlessly
going nowhere. But shining.
With shiny eyes. Like brass buttons
on daddy's old military suit.

You are getting sleepy. You are getting very sleepy.

Think about sponges in the deepest
part of the ocean, where there's never
any light, advises my New Zealand friend.
Imagine being one cell inside one of those sponges.
In a soupy matrix of sponges.
Surrounded by your sisters, by
a billion molecules of sea water.

Like a sensory deprivation chamber.

How can you stay alert
in all that darkness?

I don't know.
But I do. I stay awake all night.

Train. Camels. Sponges. New York.
Paris. Rome.

72

Quick! Into the submersible. We're going down.
Down into the darkness.
Will we come back up?
That depends.
On what?
The sponges. How much they want from you.

And the camels?
We'll load them up with baskets
and put them in the box car.
Clickety-clack. Clickety-clack.
Across the Sahara. And we won't come back.
Plateau of Tademait. Tuat Oasis.
Sebba. Murzuq. Wadi Halfa.
Carrying brides. Carrying water
in our camel-skin bags.

Yellow Room

In a yellow room—but the walls are not
painted yellow nor the furniture, it is not the citron light

of afternoon in a postmodern novel. It emanates
from the air itself, as though an idea, crammed full of electrons,

were spinning there. In some ways I suppose you might call it
a conventional room—lovely arched windows set back in deep white

walls, terra cotta tiles on the floor cool to the touch, but no ceiling.
A day room. A waiting room in a desert where it hasn't rained

for a thousand thousand years. Where a woman stares her own death
in the face. At the suddenly stilled and knotted winter light, the yellow

intensity. Date palms are noted in the distance; the sky is gorgeous,
ordinary, heart-breaking.

EUCLID

Portrait of a Blue-Tailed Skink

Skink with a blue tail poised
on the sandy edge of the ivory ceramic tile,
waiting for me to wake up
and write him into this poem.
He's happy to be in one corner like this,
while the main action occurs
elsewhere.

Elsewhere is the stunning salt water
that makes up the Pacific, its heaving glitter,
its lacy white borders, its bad
manners and raucous night noises.
Right here, it does what oceans do best:
staggers us with its power. Gives us coral, oysters
and deep sea fish with outlandish lamps
for reading Rilke undercover at night.

A green and white striped leaf
waves fitfully in the afternoon sea breeze,
pointed tip quivers
as though unhinged. What does daily life
mean to a leaf, a blue skink,
or one crashing Pacific wave?
I'll tell you what it means:
untroubled by conflicting desires.

Margarita's Story

In her sunken garden, the strangler fig
cracks the pot and lifts muscled branches
up through the black grille. In the *llanos*
it would be smothering a palm.

So when a Venezuelan friend refers to an entwined couple
as a *matapalo*, I can feel the man
taking all the available light
from his lover, his chlorophyll molecules
pulsing and trembling to grow, grow!

The ceramic wind chimes attached to the fig
twirl very slowly
back and forth, making no sound.
Yet watching them one is mildly expectant,
a little irritated at the dull silence.

Then it's evening and the tiny frogs hop up
out of the watery cups of the bromeliads.
They love the dark
upright piano Margarita plays every evening
and when the piano tuner comes once a month
to manipulate the hammers and strings and small screws
that come undone in the moist air

the frogs, perhaps imagining him to be
an odd species of their own kind,
begin to sing like a Greek chorus,
lamenting some amphibian tragedy
louder and louder
until he trembles, telling them to shut up
he has work to do
but they don't shut up.
They're going to sing all night.

Between Tofino and Ucluelet

Whenever I try to describe myself at 18,
living in a small house I built
from plastic, driftwood, rope and nails
on the west coast of Vancouver Island
between the small fishing towns of Tofino and Ucluelet
before it became the Pacific Rim National Park,
people's eyebrows raise slightly,
I sound so, well, *eccentric*.

No clothes. Fasting, sometimes, for days.
Gathering beautiful navy blue mussels
for a feast on the beach one night,
unable to eat them because
they had been so recently, tangibly, *alive*.
Singing a bivalve lament only I could hear.

I wore seaweed braided into my long black hair.
Danced with my shadow on the beach
when the shimmering heat made hallucinations
at the water's edge,
and it was hard not to just plunge in and swim,
maybe forever, drifting on sapphire waves of light
all the way to China.

There were men, too. Other lost souls.
Wanting things from me I couldn't have given anyone, then.
Men I couldn't bear to touch.

One who licked live ants off his forearms
and ate them, smiling and crunching,
chanting, *protein, protein…*

And the twin brothers who said the same thing simultaneously
so often we treated them, finally, as a single entity.

A couple whose long blonde hair was so intertwined
they never went anywhere alone.

I was very thin. One long electric nerve ending.
Making starts of conversations
that hung a long time, unanswered, in the dripping air.
Unable to stay through the winter rains. Unable
to stand in any place longer than the blink of an eye
or else paralyzed, in a trance.
Feeding the moon.

Saunas at midnight when we floated away from the earth,
briefly, and languished among the bright mysterious stars
of the Milky Way, hammered into the black night sky
like the shiny relics of long-dead saints.

There was a triangle of immense trees
inland, past the deer meadow and the incandescent
patches of moss and wild-flowers.
When I sat precisely in the middle
in the warm, motionless, molten afternoons
I was in a force field of living light
I have never experienced since.

One night in a bar I told everything
to somebody I'd never seen before,
and it all got tangled up
with Joanie Baez singing *Diamonds and Rust*
and my failed suicide attempt
and being raped on the highway hitch-hiking
back to Montreal that same year,
the subsequent abortion, nothing
is ever really forgotten, is it.
So we drank more gin and tonic,
and my new friend's stories began to blend right in...

I could have lived there forever.
One rainy day in October
I packed my father's old heavy canvas backpack
and hiked the long muddy trail up among huge silent trees,
pausing at the top where the abandoned radar station
used to be, surveying one last time
the wind pouring in off the sea
like a prayer,
then walking to the island highway
to get to the ferry and the grim rain-slicked streets
of the rest of the world.

Trop de Vert

I am writing all this down—sheared asphalt,
groves of mango and saman,
two white crosses moored by the highway,
side-by-side, ripe with symbolism,
but someone else's.

Also noting the names freshly painted in black
and the crimson and amber flowers spilling
over ochre earth.

In memory.

As we descend behind an orange-tarped truck,
surrounded by exuberant, ravenous green.

A bust of the virgin, painted vivid blue and yellow,
looking startled,
emerges from a chartreuse wall over a doorway.

A doorway bordered entirely with minute hand-carved stars.

Fits nicely with the two crosses,
thinks the cortex.

Trop de vert, demasiado!
insist the interneuron connections.

While the living flames of poinsettia,
unbearably bright, burn a hole
in the middle of my forehead.

Equatorial Light

The day is one long overexposure:
white fields, drained of colour
by northeastern heat, the pale
green hands of *Opuntia*
clapping above sandy-coloured soil.

At the periphery something
long-necked and white
rushes in from the *cerrado*.
Always these things come at me from the left,
from twisted barren places, desperate
for water, for the pencil thin point
my shadow makes. This time,
it's a dwarf white giraffe, an albino snake
doing the samba, an egret
swallowing a flute.

Afternoon's long slanting light restores
colour—apricot and maroon—so the fields
break into flames. Then the grey ash,
displaced snowflakes.
Then darkness. The white thing
rushes away like a little whirlwind.

Beyond Las Nieves

It's late afternoon, the sun's not setting yet,
but you feel in the cooling air how soon it will, and how soon
these trails will get dark, too dark to hike back down

without a flashlight. You have been telling me of a climb
with a fractured ankle in northern Borneo, just because
you had to make it to the top of some peak and I

stop, breathless, as you climb higher and higher.
I am paralyzed by the view of Caracas, so many metres below us,
by the dry smoking hills that surround us completely,

and by the knowledge that we cannot get any closer
to each other than this. Last night in a dream
my bedroom was suffused with a deep peacock blue.

A thick stream of sunlight spilled from a latticed window
and began to move across the Persian rug
like a large sulphur butterfly.

A wedding party arrived at the door but the man in it
wasn't you, or anyone I recognized.
A young girl handed me flowers—yellow *araguaney*

mixed with musky *bucaré*,
and a set of ornate 19th century keys.
I placed the bouquet

into that stream of sunlight
and it stayed there, in the air, as though I'd put it
on the smooth surface of a lake, water so clear

I could see every detail of the Persian rug
5 metres below. The keys sank immediately,
flashing bronze and silver, twisting.

Patty Larkin Live

I wanted to write a fan letter to Patty Larkin but I was feeling inhibited.
Dear Ms. Larkin, I thought, shuffling my feet and folding and unfolding
my long slender fingers like origami, I just wanted to say how much I
appreciated your edginess and fine sarcastic sense of humour. You
remember how the lighting was lavender and magenta and your hair had
a curious purple glow—whatever that stuff is you put in your brain, I'd
like some the next time you come to town. People were riveted in place.
No one got up and danced, we were all too mesmerized by the deep blue
light emanating from your guitar. It slowly filled the church and began to
spill out into the street. People walking by thought there were UFOs
attacking the church so they called the police. The windows of the
church turned royal blue and finally someone in the audience began to
clap and the blue pulsed along with the clapping and then the song
stopped and no one else saw you levitate just in that split second before
you cracked a grin but I did.

Zebras in Vermont

Mid-February and I'm listening to Ottmar Liebert again, at ear-splitting volume. A bad sign. Better though than succumbing in despair to the lack of light. Better than taking melatonin and standing on my head waiting for my pineal gland to implode. Put your ear to the page. Go on. You can hear the sounds of February in Vermont if you just make a little effort. The ice cracking and shifting on Lake Champlain. The fish beneath the ice, baiting the ice fishermen and women. Snow falling through evening shadows. Zebras galloping hither and yon across the snowy fields. With abandonment. A whole herd of them, kicking up their heels. *The time-space continuum again*, I sigh, ringing the little hand bell I keep by the door. The zebras are gone in an instant, but their hoofprints remain, across the fields and hills, indigo and dark purple, bruises in the snow. Maybe it's just the melatonin. Or it could be February, mystical as usual. Today the sun went down like the fallen petals of orange-pink gladioli, leaving curious stains on the snow. Which might be imagined to be fading zebra stripes.

Vallejo

He lived in a deep dark dazzle, Paris, 1938,
the months before death, near the catacombs—a dangerous

abyss, into which rain fell continuously. It was spring,
but the flowers were brittle and the famous park vicious,

the statues grey and dank, almost treacherous.
The depth of things was too deep!

Hot black. Deep red. Spain, Spain with her torn ballet skirt
and painted pointy shoes, killed him centimetre by

centimetre. Paris was somnambulant; he never slept.

Euclid

for R. T.

Euclid, walking on tiptoe on switchblades
in the town dump, was staring down some vultures

on his way to the city lights. *Geometry, my dear,*
said one. The yellow sands of the Gobi Desert

began to blow in his ear. A palm tree sailed by,
and then a small battered car. The railway

tracks watched him with their grey antiparallel eyes.
Triangles entered his house through

the closed windows, leaving him breathless. *The lilacs
will tell you everything*, they said.

L'Esprit de Corps

*How about being reincarnated
as a showy pink peony?* he asked.
The golden girl nodded her assent,

too confused to say, *Not now.* If we
were in Bali we could climb the sacred
mountains and keep on going,

straight into paradise. Paradise
is an island, he said, in parentheses.
Not like Ohio. Ohio in December is

flat and dreary, she knows this,
has studied geography and is terrified
of being that far away from one coast

or another. In case of a bomb or war.
In case of the need to escape by sea
or air. She thinks of paradise

only in terms of safety. Safety in numbers,
safe house, don't forget
to wear a safe, she reminds him,

thinking of a combination.
She's so full of *esprit de corps*
she'd consider being tied up

in silk scarves or blindfolded with raw
eggs pouring slowly down her breasts:
erotica. She prefers exotica, the paranormal,

get it while you can, her own brand.

Poem Beginning with a Line from Sharon Thesen

A light snow falling in the room.
Woman dancing slowly in a black silk dress.

The jaguar in the Rousseau painting
stretches and yawns, tail twitching.

Pomegranates and watermelon at two
in the morning. Constellations she'd

pinned to the ceiling, a greenish glow
like the northern lights in miniature,

not repelling the pain of living. Nor the
bottle of good red wine. Winter weather

advisory on the radio, static in the room.
This poem wants some red in it, either blood

or a valentine, oh the end of love, the woman
with the moon she's slowly circling.

Watching snow fall she is spellbound.
The big cat comes in from the cold,

curls up at her feet, the radio moves on.

Alegría

Alegría, alegría, sings Mercedes Sosa,
her voice vibrant, resonant as a
falling star in the desolate night

sky. This morning it snowed and out my
window was a picture of rural
Vermont. I am *Slouching Towards Bethlehem*,

I wear dark glasses, and
a simple linen shift. I walk and walk
the deserted beach

where nothing grows but rocks.
The islands merge into mist,
the lake is a grey membrane, diaphanous

but dangerous. Oh the sharks, the ravenous
sharks, rolling in the green breakers, grinning
their toothy grins. When I lie down,

a voice says, *Your father is dead.*
I get up, read the newspaper. Snow today, more
snow tomorrow. Lovely saffron petals

fall from the mouth of my Indonesian frog mask.
Its eyes follow me around,
the room slowly recedes.

In the Here and Now

This is happening on a Caribbean island,
one of many. Pain here is reflexive.
Also sedation, sun, the violence of

tiger lilies and stinging nettles.
Nabbed by joy, she is robbed point-
blank. Having little cash, she offers

her favourite silver earrings, which
the thief puts between gold teeth, snaps in half.
Don't step on the coral, don't

eat the raw fish. She tries to focus on
weighty matters: write the alphabet
backward and in Russian. Great poems

will surely come of this. Ah, Akhmatova,
Yesenin! In this landscape of brittle stars
and mangroves, the epic poem eludes her.

What she needs is huge wind-swept plains,
horses pulling brilliant red sleighs
across snowy fields, the anguish of

Chekhov and his suicidal sisters. She's
got a white panama hat, a passion
for midgets and tall angular transvestites,

little else. Land crabs, sweet well water.
The sign painted on the gaudy red and green bus
saying *Fuck me senseless.*

In Russia

The boy stood by the woodpile. Small, handsome,
black hair, grey eyes. Thought he was following

a unicorn into a field of goldenrods. Heard the strain
of a violin, faintly. Asked the old man

Is that the new musician, Tchaikovsky?
The old man shook his head, took out a pipe which he lit,

cautiously, back to the wind, and the palace.
The woodpile harboured spiders, traitors, spies.

The boy could smell them on the evening air.
Was something buried there?

From a Courtyard in Guatemala
I Can Almost See Rome

Spring in Rome I can barely imagine—
the impressions, second-hand
through your letters, the warm caress
the Italian sun makes of your skin,
like nylons hugging a leg
or an elbow-length kid-leather glove
worn to be shown-off
by a night-club girl,
whose dance routine demands such innuendos,
apparently unrehearsed gestures,
the glove a snake
sliding down the cool forearm
for the black-suited men in shadows,
grotesque with brandy and stubby cigars,
whose own wives find them caricatures
of the young men they married
all those centuries ago.

In the rain in Guatemala
white lilies droop
and I inhale the cacophony
of a thousand roses,
their conflicting scents overwhelming
in tangerine, ivory, *amarilla*.

Here, everyone's into cocaine,
long white lines
like the ones on the highway
that tell you where the edges are
but not how to get off them,
or how fast you can go.

You listen for your Keats
in the rain-soaked air.
I half-expect a glimpse
of my father, who came here
20 years ago after a wild ride
through Colombia on horse-back,
looking for a mythical silver mine.

His footsteps in front of me
like something Leakey might have unearthed,
an *Australopithecus*,
destination unknown.

Icebergs on the Río Doradas

This is my first winter away from snow and ice storms
and blue clouds of breath obscuring my face
whenever I step outside.

This is my first winter in the south.

Between two trees, I swing in a hammock
facing the crooked smile of a crescent moon
while flashes of lightning bugs
define the spaces between branches and leaves overhead.

The lizard with its beautiful jewelled neck
sunbathes daylong flat
against the flattened stones,
sleeps in its hole under the porch.

Hundreds of beetles and moths and tiny flies
circle the lights that send arcs or SOS signals
out into the humid dark.

Deliver me into snow.
Scotch pine and alpine fir laden with it.
A landscape blue with snow shadows,
the first blizzard of the season.

Put some frost on these thin glazed windows of light.
Send me snow in the mail.
Enough to go skiing
between the *zapote* trees and the mango branches
and the tall green shoulders of maize.
Some for snowballs to explode
the magenta sensuality of banana flowers.
Snowdrifts to cover the fields,
the blazing red of chili plants.

And down the *Río Doradas*
among the upturned roots of bamboo and palm
icebergs to float immense, impossibly alien, dream-like.

Beauties on Mad River

for Naomi Chesler

Vistas of the floating world in all directions—
drive down HW 17 in Vermont in June after a thunderstorm
or in early morning cloud and mist:
sensual blues of mountains and a glimpse—briefly—
of frivolous beauties hitching up their kimonos
to climb the Appalachian Gap, arriving late
at the One Heart Festival
fans fluttering, paper parasols overhead.

Waiting for their patrons outside the Rainhouse
famed for its cooling mists and cherry garcias,
they murmur quietly,
pale skin an object of curiosity no less than their
vermilion undergarments.

Still waiting as the grapefruit moon softly rises and softly
shines, they cross the snow geese bridge,
take a wooden boat down the Mad River,
astonishing the solitary night fishermen
with their paper lanterns and the red lacquered
gates open invitingly at the bow.

Seahorse Key

There is no other way to explain how we do this:
we census horseshoe crabs, counting
the numbers of males and females, whether single or
in pairs, noting the percentage of the carapace covered with barnacles
and whether each crab has been previously tagged,
writing all this information on a data sheet
attached to a clipboard
protected from the intermittent rain with plastic
that flaps and gets in the way, using pencils that break easily
in the damp salty air...

Inside the stone lighthouse
at the top of the hill
everything is dazzling white,
even in the rain on a cloudy day,
except the wooden floor, painted jade green—
a mere whim of the painters

or meant to simulate grass (there is none on the island).
The effect is surreal, like a Dalí painting,
as if there should be hooded or cloaked women
hovering above the horizon.

Instead, we have brown pelicans
nesting in the low trees,
those masters of subliminal grace, preening and squawking
like a crowd of hung-over angels—

no book on the beauty of the unconventional
would be complete
without a pelican as centrefold—

unless perhaps it contained the astonishing helmets
of the coupling horseshoe crabs, half-buried
in sand or out and about,

swimming in tandem like railways cars—
ancient, poorly understood, gloomy,
also in peril, also alien, also
in their element, as we stagger to carry them
from water to earth, we who can be tranquil
neither place.

When We Begin to Burn

for Richard Summerbell

I

What can I learn about your childhood
in the Similkameen from the inside
of an office of a grey stone building
in Toronto? You collected wildflowers
and mushrooms, ended up a biologist.
No one was surprised.

As a boy you spent hours
perched on hillsides—imagined
being alive before the dinosaurs.
All the layers of rock—rust and buff,
thin streaks of metal
like gold thread through a silk blouse,
and the sagebrush making dry heat,
dust reducing colour
to dull brown & grey.

You were an airplane, a bush pilot
who rescued men on ice floes
lost in the unexplored north.
Disguised as Huckleberry Finn,
I went south,
following my father.
He didn't recognize me.

In what I know of you in high school
there's a gap. Tell me about
the man you fell in love with.

I had just met a woman who would
leave me in a bar in Montreal.
She overwhelmed me.

I was transparent,
glided inches off the ground.
Even learned to walk through walls.
Hoped there was a clearing someplace

beneath dark green pine:
the one you and your lover lay in.
I imagined the last wildflowers
blooming with a romantic brilliance
but you say the fall
in these mountains is a time
of small soft colours, fungi and dying grasses.

II

It was I who wore a moustache
to the costume party.
You don't pretend anything—
the blue and white kimono
flows down your frame,
a waterfall when you move.

The white woman dressed as Othello the Moor
knows exactly where she fits.
The deep-sea diver asks you to dance—
he isn't prepared for a yes.

When the devil asks
if we're men or women,
we bow and answer in Japanese,
whisper into our sleeves.

Everglades

We take the tourist ride around Florida Bay on a pontoon boat mid-morning, the fog has lifted, the tide is turning, and there are cormorants and great blue herons and pelicans congregating on the mud flats, feeding time all day. The fish chug along through muddy waters, maybe they'll end up in the beak and down the gullet, part of bird muscle and feathers and alert, watchful eyes. We listen to stories of the keys, the near extinction of egrets for their fashionable plumes, how men escaping "The Law" used to disappear in the labyrinth of the Everglades. The man who experimented with breeding goats on a key and who, when he ran out of fresh water, tried to train them to drink the ocean. Everyone's abuzz when the loggerhead turtle surfaces nearby and then swims across the bow, its powerful green flippers pushing back the water, moving forward to feed or mate or lay its packet of eggs, who knows? *A European tourist shot and killed in Miami yesterday*, grumbles the proprietor of the fruit stand, home of the most southern purple martin house in the United States. *If only we had some kryptonite*, my companion mutters, *we could save the Everglades and zap the cane growers and developers and tourist-killers, send them to Mars for awhile.* What amazes me is the calm demeanour of the great blue heron, his stately walk, then how long he stands motionless, waiting for a little silver flash of protein to accidentally swim within range. Such a fish is headed straight for heaven.

Under the River

Every time last week I stood up to my knees
in the cold river water
and looked up into the yellow cathedral of leaves
I could feel the air on my face,
its thoughts of blizzards and blue winter winds
coming south from Hudson's Bay
and streaming off the Great Lakes

and my feet were squishy
and numb in my shining black boots
and I thought of the dragonfly nymph
hunkered down in the gravel underwater
opening and closing the deadly brown elbow
of its underjaw
grasping stoneflies and yanking
young unsuspecting caddisflies right out of their
twiggy, pebbly cases, even attacking minnows
finning their way leisurely up or down the stream,

how that nymph will stay all through the winter
down in the pebbles getting imperceptibly
bigger and fatter, its wing pads
slowly but surely preparing themselves
for the spring launching, straight up into the warm
green air, fragrant with wildflowers!

I wonder what it would be like,
under the ice, in the cold stream
all winter, guarding that perfect predatory
body, so agile and wicked and complex
and built to last no more than a year.

Camille Claudel

Bill in snake boots stalks the Green Swamp
for the pitcher plant filled with mosquitoes

and other small aquatic denizens which could,
if one were starving, be eaten as snacks, raw.

We laugh this off but Camille Claudel wouldn't have.
Hiding in her apartment sculpting the brilliant images

of her own mind falling into deeper water, no stars
in sight, nothing to eat. We are served fried this and that,

don't ask too many questions. The single channel on TV
offers Liberace. Rodin heard Camille's voice thin as paper

in the dark leaves, the Gates of Hell tarnished,
but blazing, her passion.

The Last Word

The pale gossips whisper in the corner.
The heavens are not moved. Pluto is still the ninth planet

but its status is doubtful. I know where it will fall to earth
streaking the heavens in an apocalypse of fiery reds

and blues. I've seen it in the long rectangular
reflecting pools of the Taj Mahal velveteen nights

when the moon is a thin crescent, where Gandhi walked
pensively, murmuring to himself beloved mantras

and wondering if it was Pluto, great God of the lower
world who arranged for his death. *Bah*, say the gossips,

Don't waste your time. We've got a juicy tidbit about
that fancy French sculptor, Rodin. But Camille glides in

and completes the bronze job in an instant, capturing their
expressions and shutting them up for good.

LAMENT

Western Ireland

We stroll hand-in-hand along narrow cobbled streets
between rows of slate-grey houses and small shops.
You are brown and healthy-looking

after a summer in Sardinia. I have just seen
a Harold Pinter play in which the woman, undone
by the man's infidelities, rather than murdering him,

his lovers, etc., swallows her anguish, becomes heroic,
and writes complex short stories about multiple relationships
in a third woman's voice. Outside Limerick

sunlight drenches the iron gates to a graveyard
the colour of apricots and orange blossoms.
A clump of tiger lilies burns the air. I cannot

live like this. In a twilit field, after a greasy dinner
of haddock and chips, we discover a wooden post
with four spurs embedded in it, as though left

by four horsemen contemplating which direction to take
at the end of the world. Later, I lie beside you, sleepless.
I examine the doilies beneath the lamps,

the cracks in the wall above the brass headboard.
The glass door-handle disperses splinters of light
that lodge under my fingernails like bamboo.

Electra

When did we first become aware
of out father's buttocks,
the startle of real legs poking out
below a bathing suit
after all those decades of grey flannels,
the crease my mother ironed
until the knees grew shiny
and I could see in them
the faint outline of my father's bones?

It was when I grew frightened of him,
midnight, at the icebox, rumpled
and smelling faintly of rum, faintly
of something else.

The definition of sexual, male, other
kept me glued to my chair for hours,
reading books about lost worlds, jungles,
that golden city in the Andes
flanked by cloud forest and mountains.
The books were his gifts, the wall
erected between my father and me,
the eldest daughter,
and all the time he traveled
I was tunneling,
trying not for the womb
but the first cells,
seeds from outer space.

Like meteorites whose outer shell
burns up hitting the atmosphere
of earth, parts of us lodged
in the dark soil, the gardens.

Fucking my first man
I went crazy over the details.
I thought he could give me back
my father, fingerprint
by fingerprint.

Celluloid

All the young boy whores
in flickering streets
pout their lips and prowl,
there's that arch in their spines,
sullen part in their hair.

If we could be that clear
about our needs. If only the lean
line of a body, sex in the afternoon
could rid me of the man whose black hair
falls into his eyes, who smokes in the red exit light
of some all-night dive,
slouched against grimy walls.

To seduce me, he conjures
my father's house—a simple trick
to make our affair
illicit as the crimes he tallies up,
bloodhound on the trail of lust,
that's how he found me
and why I followed him here, pure instinct.

Inside the house his jacket opens—
ivory breasts startle my mouth
like amaryllis. The nipples
are a dissolving into poppies,
flashbacks of gardens.

I wake up to my skin, that monogamous bitch,
won't let me touch even myself,
the girl in a white tutu
who puts on rubber mud-caked boots,
binoculars, climbs a tree in the rain

to view both sides of the moon:
Cleopatra or Marilyn Monroe
poisoned one way or another
and raised from the dead
in celluloid.

Fire and Water

I cast the *I Ching* before I left for México
and it said we were incompatible
as fire and water.
(I am talking about a relationship
that began like a Roman candle giving off sparks
of multi-coloured light.)

In Tuxtla, we stayed with friends
who were kind and hospitable and very American.
In their living room was a Van Gogh
with a background of emerald and indigo grass
and a bowl of irises that glittered in the mid-day heat
as if cut from cellophane.

In the nearby market there were hundreds of varieties
of orchids and many thin and excitable children
and a wooden corral built to hold
a truckload of watermelons.

Such fecundity, and the children, because they weren't ours,
seemed angelic, or at least not plotting assassinations,
though it's a statistical fact that excessive energy
comes from a poorly balanced diet, *demasiado azúcar*,
but the watermelons, bursting out of their corral,
sang in their cool pink tongues, crooning
birth, birth, the black slippery seeds
scattered among the cobblestones...

So when we drove to Sumidero Canyon,
I wanted to throw myself off the edge
like the many obsessive lovers before me.
It wasn't death by drowning
the *I Ching* predicted but the pact
I made to outlive my mother,
to outlive her suicide at 54.

From the balcony below our bedroom window
we could see a pomegranate tree
and the brilliant crests of birds-of-paradise
nodding against a lemon wall
where we drank *cerveza* until dawn
and conversed intelligibly in the end
only with the Amazonian parrot.

Landscape with Moon and Snow

We stayed with your family that first Christmas
we were together and when we couldn't take it any more
we borrowed a car that belonged to one of your many brothers,
we were both too drunk to be driving
but it was late and no one was on the highway.

As we turned down the snow-and-gravel road to the old quarry,
you reached over and flicked off the car lights.

Everything glowed white
as though in the aftermath of a huge explosion.
The midnight blue shadows of willows
criss-crossed the road like lines on the palm
of a hand: telling nothing.

We got out and stumbled through snow up to our thighs
to the edge of the grey and white

and suddenly we were teen-aged and high
and it was a hot summer night,
we were awkward, not knowing how to touch,
so we dared each other to jump
down into the green mineral pool,
the green of newly unfurled box elder leaves,
and deeper down the intense green
of the skin of iguanas,
and below that, where we couldn't see,
a blue-green which is the colour earth looks
from the edge of the galaxy—

We were poised there on the rocky shelf,
gathering together muscles and nerves,
imagining the wonderful relief
of cool green water,

poised there, stalling above the dark ice
we couldn't see the bottom of.

Sublimation

Mineral green of new leaves,
so thin light pulses through unaltered
as it does through a woman
verging on *satori*. Or madness.
She is an x-ray, a blossom
of bones, each molecule of skin jostling—
an astral projection, an obsession
of a man not her father but archetypal,
not sinister but remote,
countering the green.

And the man, the red of sumac
she finds already in August
along McCaul Street, herald of changes.
The colour of a supernova,
her heart bulges and contracts
like thunder in a sudden summer storm,
the market pungent, scented with a dozen perfumes,
watermelon and peaches, black seeds she spits out
recalling the games of childhood,
and then the other, hard pit split open,
peachlight.

Ice Fishing

We drove into a snowstorm, west, into
the heart of Minnesota. Once when
I stopped the car to watch the snowflakes
committing *harakiri* against the windshield
I had the sensation that the car was flying
over vast fields of sugar cane in bloom.

Half-way to your family home we stopped
at a silver and chromium bar
where the grenadine in our drinks was the
sun rising or falling outside
the steamy window. Maybe we should have
gotten on two planes headed in opposite
directions then, but we didn't.

The rug was a vast aquamarine ocean I couldn't
navigate in the morning.
During the night I told you I'd never
loved anyone quite like this before.

Every time lovers say this to each other
another iceberg falls off its parent glacier
and migrates south in a warm current,
becoming a haven for flocks of beautiful
blue and silver birds which then move on,
the iceberg getting smaller and smaller and smaller...

After meeting your parents I took the car
to the lake where everyone was ice fishing.
I drove across the frozen surface
dotted with a suburbia of small wooden shelters
wishing suddenly a huge crevasse would appear
that I could accidentally drive into.

Rockets

Once I answered the front door and I was wearing nothing but I was holding a huge woven palm leaf in front of me in case it wasn't you. Remember? It was a last ditch effort to bring some romance back into the rumba or samba steps we had gotten into, me depressed and smoking too much, wearing blue-green shades and feeling like a hover fly circumnavigating a flower. Wanting the pollen. Always threatening to eat a whole cauliflower at one sitting or embarrass you by going grocery shopping and pretending to be demented. So who were we? The rental car kept breaking down, it was hot, it was some southern state or other. There was nowhere to go but the Gulf of Mexico and I'd already been there twice, washed up with the mangrove seeds and sand sharks with skin like #3 sandpaper. Where else could we go? Straight up off Cape Kennedy with one of those rockets, such a parody of July 4th or 1st, I forget which war or revolution or anti-confederation we were celebrating. Anyway we could see the fireworks from the balcony through the pines and maple trees and I finally understood you were never cut out to be my one true love.

Dans les Cantons de l'Est

Last night we slept in a clapboard room. Even now
I try not to dismiss the sound your voice makes
when you wake up drunk and exhausted.

We ate grilled cheese sandwiches and fries
at 3 AM and I drank a vanilla milkshake
secure in the belief that a lack of calcium

is one of the things responsible for this
universal angst driving us into days and nights
that refuse to separate into light, dark.

We walk along frost-heaved asphalt to the silver
post-modern sculpture that doubles as a look-out
tower. Bright orange marigolds bloom

miraculously underfoot. I could not prepare you
for the way the town has been devoured by the pit,
Hôtel Québec and the pool hall

I spent my adolescence in, transformed
into this thin and glaucous air
above yellow dump trucks moving rock

from one side of the pit to the other, the street
I lived on with its huge ancient shade trees
ending in a chain-link fence and a sign,

No Trespassing. I lived here on the periphery for seventeen years
but now I live in dusty motel rooms.
I will be waking to unfamiliar ceilings in Chiapas,

Patagonia, Guatemala City, London
with you or without you.

Texas

I went back to western Texas,
to Big Bend National Park, once, alone.

It was after we'd split up, and were again capable
of civilized conversations.

No more smashed bottles of Jack Daniels, no more taking
each other's entire record collections
and dropping them, album by album,
off the balcony of a room in the Marriott
Hotel in San Antonio. No more insane driving
through a graveyard at 2 AM in a blizzard
playing chicken with the hidden stones.

I want to see again that motel room in Marathon,
north of the Chisos Mountains,
where we watched the iridescent butterflies
that had been painted on the wall
lift off and one by one drift out through
the open door into the weak autumn sunlight.

I want the motel owners who immigrated here
from Calcutta to offer us, again,
a magnificent lunch of curry
because our rental car has inexplicably broken down,
because they are homesick for India and cannot
comprehend America,
and because the motel is at the edge of a landscape
where the wind passes through everything
without mercy.

Love as a Moving Object

Listening to Kate Bush on the slow
early morning drive to work
past the huge oaks and bright pink houses on 6th Street,
past a disgruntled man in black leather
pushing his dysfunctional Harley along the sidewalk,
it's going to be at least 90° in the shade,
and Kate is singing in her passionate, articulate way
about being in love
and never getting out of it...

We all know what that means.
It means to be stalled, trapped,
stuck—because love is a moving object,
like a duck to a duck hunter
who wakes up at early and dresses
in prickly long underwear and hip waders,
shivers in the pre-dawn light, the clouds
racing, scattered and eerie overhead,
who gets cramps in his legs, who needs
desperately to sneeze, who strains to see
that fine line dividing water from air,
he listens acutely for their telltale calls,
keeps concentrating *out there*,
focused on the weather, the ducks' weather,
he is like a man
who is very attentive to women,
who gives the illusion of intimacy
without the intimacy,
the way the duck hunter takes such good care
of his beautiful hand-painted decoys
and guns,
the way he savours every sweet mouthful
of roast duck, later, after he has carried

the handfuls of warm dead bodies
by the necks and flung them
into the back of his pick-up truck
and called it a day.

The Side Effects of Marriage + Malaria

A postcard arrives from you of Colorado mountains
—I forget which ones—
announcing your impending marriage.

The same day I examine my red blood cells
through a microscope in Caracas
and discover malaria parasites.

This is not cause and effect,
exactly, but like that violent summer thunderstorm
that began the instant my car broke down—

some events don't appear to be random.

The next morning, after a massive dose of chloroquine,
I tried walking up a long hill. Was it grief
that made me lie down
among the fallen purple petals of *Clematis*?

I have never lain down on anything
so soft.

Behind the purple radiance
the spotlights of yellow day lilies
were heating the place up, altogether
too bright.

When I closed my eyes I was lifted, vibrating,
a few centimetres off the earth.

I felt exultant, that I could be free—
and in the next breath
that nothing had changed.

Then the fever and chills began.

Lament

The time is two in the morning. The fog is
legendary. Over my right shoulder, the frayed silks

of a waterfall. A large white lily blossoms
from a crack in the wall. The earth trembles.

My lover has run away with a beauty from Mojú.
Such enchanting breasts, such crow-coloured hair!

I climb Mt. Mansfield, I bring the season's hurricanes
all the way up the northeast coast. The crème caramel

half-moon rises only to hear my lament.

Pôrto Velho

When we began everything between our bodies
was perfect.

A year later we sit in striped folding chairs
overlooking the glazed Madeira River
and sip the sweet fizz of *guaraná*.

Huge dark wasps dash themselves
against the sticky walls of our white plastic cups.
A flock of parrots shrieks and disappears
into the haven of a mango tree.

The loudspeaker blares Procol Harum's
A Whiter Shade of Pale
which is incomprehensible yet provocative, the way
as a teen-ager I imagined sex
would get easier
as I got older.

Under our table,
pools of turgid water
slowly dry to a thick paste.
The odour of urine and rotting guavas competes
with the wet river smell.

The river banks are grey and muddy
and the vegetation in the flat early afternoon light
is uniformly dull. Below us
a cartload of oranges
spills onto the brick-red earth,
the way your body used to spill itself
so effortlessly into mine.

Exposure

I like to think of you as a teenage boy
living in a large house somewhere in the southern states,
slipping out of your bedroom window after midnight,
naked as a shoestring,
walking across the grass
as if it were an open space in Africa
and you a Masai warrior with a long straight spear
and strange markings on your face.

You head for the tall oak and pine forest
where the glint of metal glimpsed among the many tree trunks
slender as the bodies of antelopes
draws you like water.

There is a faint salty smell not from your body,
a smell of metal fatigue from the bars worn smooth
by the other hands here before you,
the many young men testing themselves
against this exposure to darkness,
trying to measure
everything they've been told about shame & nakedness
against the pressure of cool metal on skin,
stretching the leg muscles, the upper and lower arms,
pushing, tensing, dropping lightly to the damp earth
and springing back up toward the shapes of leaves
pinioned against the lush backdrop of stars.

And there is always the small chance that
someone hidden in the forest is looking.
Maybe it's the girl in the physics class
who wants to be an astronomer.
She'd be out on a night like this
watching the constellations
revolve and change like a mobile of diamonds.
Or maybe the girl on the next block

with her short blonde hair and her body,
awkward except when she swims—

so you climb among the intricate bars and pipes
until you hang upside down like a pupa,
your sex two purple plums
suspended below the short black tendrils,
your penis folded and withdrawn,
you put your body through its paces
to see how far it can be pushed,
you want to know whether the muscles and tendons can take it,
whatever will be handed to them in the future,

and then you pause because the wind has veered
bringing from the garden a scent of jasmine
and honeysuckle,
you look back at the house
where the porch light makes a pool
which up until tonight has always been deep
and incomprehensible,
but now you feel as if you know everything there is to know
about that house, you've taken what is has to offer
and used it over and over until it's worn
like a spoon you can no longer see your face in.

Saying Good-bye in Belém

Belém without you
is like being vertical, when one wants
to slash the horizon into
improbable zones of colour and texture.
Ten years we were lovers.

Flocks of sea green parrots
perch on the TV
and screech at the newswoman
immaculate in a golden suit, her hair
a lacquered cap, shining under the hot
spot-lights. She persists in asking
if I know her name—leaning
unself-consciously out of the
TV screen and pointing her wireless microphone
at me: *This is just a little test—*
please go ahead and spell the word
"wireless"
backward.

Sss, I think.

Don't think of you as dead—
merely lost in the desert. Enough
water, dates, camel milk. Even
a special mail-order compass.
But you won't be back this way
anytime soon. Don't wait up...

There's nothing like an overpriced fruit and nut
chocolate bar from the airport lounge
to give a little thrill—or waking
long past midnight shivering from the tyranny
of the air conditioner. If I stop writing,
I'll be tempted to jump out the

window. Ten floors down, exactly.
I counted them as I walked up
after dinner, taking the
stairs two at a time.

Loss

My former lover and I stroll for hours
the neutral, gritty sand of Daytona Beach.

Waves, sound of surf, careening jeeps. I feel only
the crunch of individual grains of sand on each cell of each foot,

cannot hear his words. Small rafts of despair bob
among the turbulent hills of waves, the rising tide. *End*

of summer, say the leaves and trees. I place a tiny sand dollar
in the pocket of my black linen dress which I find months later in another

life, pulling out summer clothes. I lick the sand dollar for the salt as a deer
would do. When I rub it across my cheek it leaves a thin red line.

The Land of the Kingfisher

The Flower Woman and the Dog Star

I'm crying, meandering the broken streets
of Caracas just before dawn, a dangerous time.
A woman in a doorway weaves petals of flowers
onto a slender frame.

She begins to tell me her version
of the story of the Dog Star,
where Sirius is so blinded by grief
because his friend the Jaguar has been killed
he cannot see his own light is fading.
And what would the sailors do, asks the woman,
if the Dog Star extinguished himself?
How would you find your way home?

We both look up instinctively
into the pre-dawn sky, now almost violet.
Behind me is the blackness where I have been lost,
even from myself.
But that is where the Jaguar is.

The Great Darkness

> To live here one must forget much.
> —Anne Carson

Two more nights of insomnia, two nights
I inhabit the dark part of the universe.

These are not the nights when the wondrous poem
comes looking for me, nor the nights

I solve any great personal mysteries or absolve
anyone of the splendid tragedies of my childhood.

These nights are bleak and seductive and so terribly
private they never make it into poems. One day

there will be a critical text "Catharsis and Personal Tragedy
in the Poems of Conn's Middle Years." I

look forward to that. I believe in the great balance
of dark and light. Meanwhile, it's late

and in my bedroom I am surrounded by my favourite
books, silk prints from Japan, a Tahitian batik on the walls,

the massive ancient butternut chest-of-drawers
inherited from my father, my palm trees wavering slightly

in the exhalations of night air, all this private memorabilia
carefully designed to combat personal devils and still

the great darkness is winning, hands down.

Immortality & Co.

Wakened out of some odd episode about a gila monster,
its orange and black stripes
no doubt making me think
about tigers (my favourite carnivores)

or maybe it was that reptilian sensuality
arousing me—I'd prefer to caress a snake
than some (ahem) men—

Anyway the gila monster was deep in conversation
with a century plant— they were discussing
immortality and Kafka...

It was a desert (of course), searing sunlight,
no oasis in sight, the century plant melancholy
(not due to flower for 25 years), wanting to know

What was the point of it all, anyway.
: Ottmar Liebart's *Nouveau Flamenco.*
Gertrude Stein in Paris. Eduardo Galeano.
Woody Allen's latest film.
Self-Portrait with Braid, 1941 by Frida Kahlo

on my bedroom wall, the necklace of dark grey skulls,
totemic faces & stones—which is what really
woke me up. The braids pulsating.
Ugly, pointed leaves in place of a dress,
the stem winding its way about her hair. Death

definitely on the agenda.
Seductive death—
not a metaphor for anything.

Threshold

On the other side of the mirror
in her parents' bedroom closet
lived the man she was always being
warned against, the one from whom
she must never accept candy or a ride
in a strange black sedan with
darkened windows, the man
also blackened as if by smoke,
at least that was how she always
saw him, at dusk, emerging from
the lower corner of the mirror,
almost like a ground fog or smoke
blown out of the lungs of a figure
in a Laurie Anderson song, making
a little pathway across the room,
one she recalls very clearly at twilight,
now that she's grown-up, she remembers
oh yes, she recalls
the shame and the after-shocks of it
but she's permanently lost the feeling of that first
hesitant step beyond the mirror.

Now she wants to undream
the whole sequence of events, working backwards.
She tries to reinhabit her own body, the abandoned
elbows, the little girl kneecaps, the sweetness
that was there before,

and can't take her back.

Francis Bacon's Roses

for Gerry Shikatani

In Paris, people were sunbathing on the cobblestone beach in front of the
Centre Georges Pompidou, washed up against mime and portrait artists and
carts of postcards and pages torn out of antique books. All the guts of the
building on the outside, functionality rather than beauty, some
fundamental rebellion against the harmony of classical lines, avenues
straight as arrows, the gracefulness of the chestnut trees, the Eiffel Tower
like a huge mechanical praying mantis. Inside the Cathedral Notre Dame
the amazing infinitude of arches and the stained glass in hues of blue and
red. It was only later that I found the Rose Window in a video-taped
conversation with Francis Bacon who was being queried about the
morbidity of his work. He said he painted what he saw, he was a realist,
true to his vision. His triptych of roses: one in the first ephemeral flush
of beauty unfolding, so convincing its pervasive perfume wafted
throughout the gallery for years afterwards; the second painting
accelerated time a bit showing the fallen petals like red hands loosened
after great extremity or prayer; the third depicting the withered rose,
edged the faint brown of sepia-tone. Of the faces he paints, many are on
slightly elevated stages as though self-conscious of their human
condition, some are contorted, others are inside open cubical structures
as if the British have come to live their lives inside a hierarchy of cages
with newspapers blown at their feet detailing the monotonous and
scandalous in ever-larger letters.

Where I Am It is Dark

I say to the array
of carved wooden animals migrating
out of my living room and onto the
back porch, *Let me sleep through the night
without dreaming.* If I read
about the Middle Ages I am sure to awaken
in one corner of an Hieronymus Bosch painting,
a pale crusader in red leotards
wondering what to do with my hands.

Send them out for a little walk...

After seeing *Postcards From the Edge*
I became the recovering middle-aged
actress, not as beautiful as Meryl Streep
but awake all night because of the movie sets
and photographers crowded into my bedroom.

Or one night after I rubbed my large
wooden tapir with toxic tung oil to preserve it
my brain sped along some private track
like a runaway train through the snowfields
of the Yukon faster and faster until it smashed
the hero of du Maurier's
The House on the Strand....

It came to a stop the next morning
at the foot of my bed, still
steaming, snow-covered.

Dog Dreams: A Fable of Waking Life in the 90s

I

The room fills suddenly with
large trained dogs. Dobermans, German shepherds,
Rottweilers. But as in a
comic book, some are russet, others
cadmium, still others, pure white.
Larger than life.

At a single word from a man
leaning in the doorway,
each woman in the room
is surrounded by a tight formation of dogs
so she cannot take a single step.
The dogs suddenly vicious,
snarling, ready to attack
on command.

II

Animals in dreams can symbolize many things.
The wounded part of the self, the playful part, the etc.
These dogs, while menacing and powerful, are coloured
like cartoons. Should this be taken as a warning
of the potential menace in ordinary-looking objects?
That dogs may be man's best friend, but not
woman's?
What would Clarissa Pinkola Estes, the analyst, say?
Would she remind us how closely dogs
are related to wolves? That we should befriend them,
imagine them as guides or interpreters?

III

Into the room strides the owner,
dressed like the leader of a cult,
shouting—commands at the dogs and
to intimidate the women.
Who is this? The dreamer's father?
One of the many guises of the self?
The woman transformed into a man
to take back the power
trickling away
in her waking life?

IV

The women can be released
only if they join the man's cult.
No one speaks or moves.
At another word of command the dogs
begin to attack the women.

If this were my dream, I'd simply levitate
out of that scene, put myself down
in an alpine valley. Glowing in the distance,
some snow-capped mountains.

V

However. The man approaches each woman, calls off
the dog and grabs her by the hips, forcing his tongue
and a slender wafer into her mouth.
As he nears the dreamer she starts screaming,
spits out the wafer,
vomits on his polished black shoes. Is thrown
brutally to the ground. Hears something crack, tear.
Wakes up.

VI

Outside, a dog barks. There are birch trees near the house,
irises in her garden, and a stream, although
for the moment she cannot hear
the sound of running water.

The Land of the Kingfisher

Willow moon lifts her fat chin over the hot plains of Zaria,
stares hard and yellow through my hotel window.

If I could just fall asleep. Just fall asleep to the rustle
of blue silk as hundreds of dancers slip in single file

past my embroidered bedspread on their way to a royal
performance. Past the Arab quarter, past the woman in white

burning incense in the shadows of a mosque, past
the gravestones and the scentless sand blowing at the outskirts

of the village. To the low violet hills where the blind emir waits,
a man whose displeasure it is dangerous to awaken.

Between One Blue-Grey Island and Another

When it happens—enlightenment, ecstasy,
whatever it's called in whatever language
I am living in by then—
I won't want to come back.

It's like that instant last night
where the lion and I were curled
in each other's arms
and I couldn't tell which was me—
fur or human skin, straw-coloured mane
or short black hair,
having lost all sense of *mine*
and *yours*
having crossed some boundary
that had been holding me inside this body
40 years.

So when it arrives at my balcony
like the wind in my wind chimes,
the chimes I bought in Colorado
to remind me of my childhood,

I will go through the proper rituals and ceremonies,
I will light my mint green candle
and the incense that smells like cinnamon
and the inside of a rain forest,

my ego will get into a small boat
and be benignly abandoned
between one blue-grey island and another.
I'll wave it good-bye sweetly.

I won't miss a thing.

Turning Back to the Green

Will you believe me if I tell you
I wasn't—well not seriously—
abandoned as a child?

And yet I dream of it—being lost, forsaken—
with great frequency.

For example: in Budapest, in a garden terrace,
eating lunch with a group of fellow-travellers.

I notice another garden, an interior one,
in an adjoining building. There's a young woman
airing sheets in a light room,
facing the overgrown, tangled green.

I watch her. She has an arresting face,
an ikon, bathed in yellow light.

There are black iron stairs,
a fire-escape, descending
into the flowers.

Flowers that are deep red, their cups
dizzyingly scented.

But I keep turning back
to the green.

It is difficult to leave.
I never speak to the girl, yet
the sense of place exerts some magnetic pull,
charming me.

When I return to the terrace, my companions have left
to catch their plane home
(though it's never clear
where that is), left their lunch
in chaos, left me.

Then I am in Spain.

 My car is being repaired by a drunken mechanic.

Most of the engine is in pieces
on a weedy, cracked sidewalk.

I peel oranges, offer him piece after piece.
Anything so he will stop taking out
just one more part.

Then I cannot find my car.

I am standing alone in front of a dark,
shuttered house
where everyone I have ever loved
has lived.

But I am surrounded
by the green.

Homage au Gaugin

pour Daniel Dussert et sa famille

So someone notices the profound influence
of certain Japanese paintings on Gauguin's life-work,
the numbers of persons per painting, the body language,
how the nuances of H's style so influenced
Le Jour des Dieux, etc. and presto, another critical contextual analysis
hits the ground, running.
That both Japan and Tahiti
were isolated islands in the Pacific, famous
for tropical storms.....

Me, I could look all day
at *Nature-Morte Aux Oranges de Tahiti*,
entering the canary-yellow background
above the pale orange tablecloth,
the oranges each luminous and shining.

Later there are seven children bathing
in the lagoon, whooping and shrieking
as they climb up onto a wooden post
and fling themselves off into the shimmering blue
and silver beneath, over and over.
Seven Tahitian children and one orange
resting on the corner
of the white wicker table
beside the faded red hibiscus. Art everywhere.

When the South Wind Comes Singing

Los esqueletos de mil mariposas
duerman en mi recinto.
                    –Frederico García Lorca

In the hour of the evening star
the south wind comes singing, drenched

with lemon blossoms.
A white peony rises like the full moon

over snow-soaked fields.
Makes me invisible, my loneliness.

These days, my heart is one part
alligator (or little lizard, frozen

by the crystalline hedge), three parts these icy
empty fields, hoping for a fox

to come loping along, all burnished
red delicate dark paws, leaping

snapping its wondrous jaws, tracking snow-mice.
Where the northern lights flirt

with the south wind.
Emerald and magenta accordions of light

explode into mango flowers,
impossible fuchsia rose petals.

And I, too, burst open,
burst into strange song...

Drunk with light comes
the southern wind, dark

and burning. The skeletons of a thousand
butterflies are sleeping in my soul.

Sea of Tranquility

Actually there are egrets and roseate spoonbills, mangroves, alligators and even, once at sunset, a glimpse of the rare Florida panther. Crescent moon and Venus. Fireflies. Another year coming, going. We can see the fiery belt of Orion, the great swath of the Milky Way. The panther could see it too, if it looked up at the stars. It would see Leo, its brother, straight overhead at this latitude in February. Playing Cat's Cradles between tawny paws. The saltwort glowed lime green along the path where we met the hissing juvenile alligator whose back was the pink of the sun setting and whose eyes were golden slits with black centres, like the entrance to the underworld. I was reading about the woman who had a heart and lung transplant and now dreams about her 19-year-old donor, who died in a car crash. Occasionally, she's driving along the highway, the car humming along at 55 and suddenly her foot jams down on the accelerator, she's 19, a sudden flush of testosterone mixed with adrenaline. Heart like a mine field. We look up at the stars one more time and they make me feel lonely, lonely for my lost childhood, all my unhappy, angry, younger selves. *Take a deep breath*, I say to each one, crowded into the elevator of the heart. *Exhale slowly through your mouth. In and out. Be a sea of tranquility.*

Roses and Stone

Dying November sun, it's dusk,
light a mauve kiss
that caresses my hands,
balanced on the black steering wheel,
misses my lips that are missing
yours so much tonight I drive
the car south for hours
in the glamorous company
of a dozen crimson roses.

Out the car window are massive cliffs
grey and white and shining like mica.
Some days I am up on the edge—

hanging by a thin rope
I glance down

or I am at the bottom
climbing, one
precarious foothold after the other,
only looking up.

Those days your face comes to me
as a rose might, newly opened,

but still I keep climbing
nervously perspiring
the view must be extraordinary
mountains mountains mountains
sea
but I am focused on stone, grey and blue
and marbled.

Hey, you knock me out, you
and the perfume these roses make,

solid as ground I can stand on.

And there, there's Georgia O'Keeffe up
on the cliff, balancing precisely
in a long skirt and cerise scarf
making a plug for sensuality and art,
a juxtaposition of stone and roses.

What I'm balanced between I can't explain,
the rose sometimes as large as a house
and carnivorous, red tiger
feasting on my anxieties. The cliffs I invent,
needing something dramatic and challenging,
my fear of heights notwithstanding.

Brockaway Gorge

Across the railway ties, across the gorge—
Don't look down.
Don't look back.
Listen to the riversong, its high green
notes. Look up at the gnarled
toes of the pines,
the stately pines that know
even the spiritually illiterate
crave illumination
by whatever means available.

Paris

A recent propensity for burning fingers—
a lack of attention to the essentials.
It sounds very Japanese, that
ritual of burning one finger at a time.
Vendredi is the thumb day, perhaps.

II

I've been down-hearted babe, ever since
the day you left—
B.B. King in back of my mind
all those days and nights of champagne
and dark chocolate in Paris. *Dimanche*
the ring-finger burning day though the fire opals
didn't arrive before the wedding
and I see them *in situ* in Australia:
ultramarine plains, mountains of rugged beauty,
but the hills of eucalyptus are in flames.

The moon rises dark and extravagant,
charmed by the flute of Rousseau.

Frida Kahlo writes on her photograph, "from your friend
who is so sad" as I sign my postcard
"from one who is so happy it tempts
fate."

III

Lying on a Louis XVI couch, surrounded by yellow
and ochre pillows,
we read passages from Camille Claudel's
diaries, overwhelmed by the green
curve of her waves, the three women
our muses, or our *Judgment of Paris*
—to the fairest, to the purest in heart, to the
sexiest

We become Kandinsky animals—elongate and turquoise.

See the world through a microscope, follow his lines of colour
to the edge of a building where a sign says **Go Back**
(but not the way you came).

Eat chocolate for what ails you
and we do that too.

IV

One of our neighbours, a political refugee, stays up later than me
listening to mournful Algerian music,
the woman's hoarse voice winding around the drums.
I see the teeth and ears of Rousseau's angel of death,
dressed in pink, astride a black horse,
flying over the battlefield of that same country.
Now the music's interrupted, the man paces overhead,
smoking one Gitanes after another, oblivious to everything
but the uncensored news.

V

In the dining room mirror at Christine and Thierry's
apartment, the streetlights behind the trees
flicker in the evening breeze, and below the clay fruit
the smile of a green-clad angel. Two candles,
pour l'atmosphere, two half-filled glasses
of red wine, and the book of Arabic calligraphy
opened at random on the letter *Lam Alif*
or the *No of Affirmation*—the letters
like musical notes we murmur in our sleep.

VI

We walk across nine bridges that span
the river and I wonder
how many people have jumped…

The Seine the colour of freshly-baked
apples, thin slices held up to the sunlight,
translucent in the August heat.

I was thinking this as I ate my *tarte aux fruits*,
I was thinking
one doesn't recover from everything.

In the film a man pulls down a blind
and the world comes unglued.

Snow Blossoms

Snow blossoms on the sundeck. Cities
of sculpted snow and ice shine from the far side

of the Connecticut River where the dead poet
John Thompson chops wood. Every morning I hear the clear

untroubled ring of his axe. Sugar maple, black
walnut, elm, alpine spruce. Secrets in the rings,

etched deep in the heartwood. The frost patterns on windows
and on the surface of shallow ponds enter his dreams

and mine too. The fragile leaves trapped there.
And the trails of coyotes chasing winter mice.

No one enters the deep forest at this time of year.
Orion, Orion! Come down

from the lit-up sky. Give John your wonderful belt
of stars; take me in your burning arms.

La Virgen de la Paz

Through her clear glass eyes,
30 metres high, all the surrounding colours
somehow focused in her eyes,
I'm peering out at the *Cordillera*,
expecting, who knows, just one
parting of the clouds, some minor miracle.

Bee-bullets of black and yellow adrenaline
mainline it for the comb
hidden up in the crevice
below the right breast. Near the dove.

What if all that energy curled up into a black
pulsating ball had nowhere to go?

And no lines on the palm of the hand,
outstretched, opening…
No future, only the bright protoplasm of the present,
pulled like a membrane,
like a polarizing filter,
over all of western Venezuela.

Look! Down there, near the mouth of
La Cueva de los Penitentes.
A patch of flattened grass, as though
someone leaped from the eyes
and landed rolling, tumbling—
fracturing both legs, cracking the rib cage…

I know someone who did that.
I know her.

Here is her house, do you see the bedroom
is a little cage, inside the cage she perches,
singing and singing…

And look, there's a sacred corner, where she brings
flowers, a pink satin fan.
Fossils of ferns and the delicate
tracings of leaf skeletons. And a white ceramic
bowl, with an aquamarine interior—
in which she might calmly bathe
on the hottest days.

Paea

Two myna birds strut up and down the lawn,
stirring up appetizers. Like they're
the owners, conversing in low, serious, yellow-legged tones
about watering the plants and trees, when.

Last night we came home late from the river valley
leaving our wet sneakers
dangling from the frangipani tree
with the moon caught between its branches.

To drift off in the middle of a thought
and be catapulted back by the orange-red
flowers in the African tulip tree.
To be ecstatic about bedroom curtains
the colour of orange sherbet. To be able to sing
but not to join the wild Polynesian dances
without hip surgery. To touch the
varnished bamboo walls on the outside of the house
and say, *Not in Vermont*. To fall in love
with the Marquisan boy who wears a
flower in his hair and has one arm
tattooed in mysterious designs of fish and octopi.
To have left behind anguish you know
will be waiting when you return.

The Ecstatic

All night, snow on the mountains.
I awake among the intricate purple shadows

of plum blossoms. River of light, bearing the ecstatic.
The man to my left with a bluebird's head is cruel and callous,

gives his neighbour the Black Death and syphilis.
Black breath. The silk of sex.

On a shoe string, he plucks a Turkish tune, his beak
nodding up and down. A bath is what I need—

a Turkish bath. The inscribed stone sweats.
Steam rising like old wishes, once cherished.

Wood and Wind

for Scott Devitte

At El Baúl the wind
is the arms of sugar cane,
sweet pulp beneath
sheaths of dense green,
the earth some great body
burning up sugar
so we feel it rising in our feet,
soft shuddering
of an earthquake in the bones.

Green sea anemone
in the grey swirl of sky,
green light,
emeralds awash with electricity:
the tree of life
through a tunnel of leaves.

It is alive the way we rarely are:
wood and wind,
point-counterpoint,
honed to the sharp edge of nothing,
where the black stone head
grins at a private joke
only the stone-carvers share.

There are angels in the wood,
you said,
and I felt their wings rustle
like leaves before a storm.

Their images resonate
backward into the wood
as ours move forward from the womb,
out into open fields.

Angels, Wind-surfing

Late one evening in Rio—after not sleeping
for 48 hours—we ate dinner in a Nile green
hexagonal restaurant
overlooking the dark, mercurial waves
of Guanabara Bay.

We had just come from a movie
where young male prostitutes lived together
like vagabonds in a derelict hotel

and then we had passed little enclaves
of transvestites, camping it up
in exotic costumes made for carnival

and street vendors who sold designer oranges
and live blue crabs tied together with string.

Maybe it was the lack of sleep
or the half-moon dangling from one corner
of an unrecognizable southern constellation—

we took the ferry across the bay to Niterói,
and there were dark blue angels wind-surfing
in the hallucinogenic ripples and deep swells of the waves—

their magnificent white wings catching the night wind,
their deep-set eyes joyous, and magical
and breath-taking...

Galileo

In Florence on a narrow cobblestone street
I stared up at the house Galileo had inhabited
and I thought how curious it was that it

was golden on the outside, like a mutant planet
or the pleased blush of an apricot, in any case
burnished in the light of August, the earth

still rotating steadily, the centre of the universe
trillions of light years away and
how close he lived, really, to the little church

at the bottom of the hill near the *Ponte
Vecchio* and how near to the stars invisibly
shimmering far away overhead. He alone could see

them in broad daylight.
They made him weep at times
although this he never recorded. I was

warned to watch for street gangs and the beggars
who work in pairs in the *Piazzale Michelangelo*;
no one suggested I look above the cypresses,

above the old Roman church *San Miniato*
on the hill, and listen for Galileo's
stars, singing in the blue hazy light of August,

when the restaurants close, line-ups
to the *Uffizi* are legendary, and *Il Duomo* stands,
green and rose and alabaster marble, dominating

the *piazza* and blocks around it, lit by moonlight,
the sky deep, mysterious blue, the Hare Krishna devotees
dancing and chanting in saffron-coloured robes

below it in the streets, I saw it glowing, I saw the stars
beginning their long dance, I felt the earth
spin and revolve on its axis, a

shiver of ecstasy. The stars' singing drowned out
the violin player in the main *piazza*
and the tourists shouting and laughing,

I was deaf to it all. Once, in August, in
Florence, I, like Galileo, heard, or imagined
I heard them sing.

Mt. Snow

On top of Mt. Snow the angels hang
upside down, a choir of albino bats.

Beneath, the river is in flood and the amber stems
of young willows can be seen moving slowly

back and forth underwater like the limbs of the drowned
or the limbs of the saved. In Jerusalem the saved

are not readily identifiable nor can one tell the religion of a temple
by examining its stones. But then the chilled watermelon

of summer floats languidly across the detonated sky.
The angels cease singing and race pell-mell down the mountain.

They jump across the river and it ceases to flood. At their passing
the willows burst into lime-green leaves; they set fire to the air.

Glossary

apamate (*Tabebuia rosea*) — native to Latin America, this tree produces an abundance of light pink flowers

arepas — typical Venezuelan food item, a small thick round bread made of corn flour and usually stuffed with seafood, cheese, avocado or meat and eaten with obligatory *salsa picante*

araguaney (*Tabebuia chrysantha*) — Venezuelan national tree which blossoms during the dry season with intense yellow flowers

barrios — slums, usually found around large cities

bucaré (*Erythrina poeppigiana*) — a native of northern South America, this large lovely tree with striking orange flowers has often been used historically to shade young coffee trees in coffee plantations

caatinga — scrub forest inland from the Atlantic coast in northeastern Brazil (between the states of Maranhão and Pernambuco)

cambur — small extremely sweet local banana, never exported

cerrado — underpopulated savannah on the central Brazilian plateau

guaraná — a soft drink tasting somewhat like a cross between cherry and apple made from the seeds of *Paullinia cupana*, with a caffeine content of 4-5%

llanos — region of west-central Venezuela, very flat and savannah-like, characterized by dry tropical forest with marked seasonality (dry/wet)

manisoba — a Brazilian meat dish

matapalo — palm and strangler fig commonly seen growing together in the *llanos*. The parasitic fig eventually kills the palm, though they may grow together for years.

Opuntia — a genus of quite common, widespread cactus — a spineless mutant is grown in northwestern Brazil for fences and cattle feed — especially important during droughts because it retains water

Popul Vuh — a document of the Quiche Indians containing legends, religion, history and traditions

Syzygium malaccense — originally from the Malayan archipelago with brilliant pink needle-like stamens and petals

Ver-o-Peso — In Belém, at the waterfront market, these scales "See-the-weight" were used to demonstrate that a customer was being treated fairly.

zapote — a fruit tree found in Central America and in northern South America, *Pouteria sapota*, with fibrous, refreshing fruit

Signal Editions Poetry Series

EDITED BY MICHAEL HARRIS

SIGNAL EDITIONS

www.vehiculepress.com